The Mountain Still Stands

A Young Soldier's Battle for Peace in a Time of War

By Meredith Mathis

Thank you to a fellow author!

Meredith Mathis

Creative Force Press

Creative Force Press

For my love, Tyler

⛰

This I know, that God is for me.

Psalm 56:9

Contents

Introduction

In December 2015, while driving to work at my active duty Army job on Joint Base Lewis-McChord, Washington, I was feeling particularly overwhelmed and hopeless about my current circumstances. After seeing almost two-dozen doctors and testing seven different medications, my nearly three-year plague with chronic vertigo was no closer to ending.

I felt abandoned by God, with no sign of my condition improving, or even getting close to a diagnosis. The Army was discharging me after almost eight years of active duty service, sending me into medical retirement. A cloud of near constant depression and anxiety had hovered over me for several months. While I drove, I cried and pounded my steering wheel, like a petulant child, wondering where God was in my suffering.

It was a gloomy and rainy afternoon, as they often are in the Pacific Northwest from October to June. Dark clouds hung in the sky, mirroring my state of mind. I made a turn down a main road on post, which on clear days offers a spectacular view of Mt. Rainier in all its snowcapped glory. But that day, nothing but a sheet of grey sky met my eyes. I honestly couldn't remember the last time I had seen the mountain. Sometimes I forgot it was there. Then, through my tears, I heard a small voice.

"How do you know the mountain is there behind the clouds?"

I automatically responded, "Because I've seen it!"

The voice replied, "You have seen me, too. I'm still here, even if you can't see me now."

My tears of pity instantly turned to tears of sweet release. I wasn't abandoned. God was still God, and He was still for me. I couldn't see the light from the dark fog of my circumstances, but that didn't change what was there, what had always been there, who will always be there. The mountain still stood. God still stood. I knew I would see the Mountain again.

This wasn't the first time in my life where hope and God and all things good seemed to be swallowed up in darkness. In fact, I distinctly remember telling God that He didn't exist, and that if He did, He was cruel. And if He was still there and still on my side, then He had better show His face and prove it. Yes, I have wrestled with God. I have run from God. I've accused Him of not being there, of not understanding, heaped blame on Him for my own shortcomings and said every other mean thing we humans are not supposed to say to God. But it's okay, because He's God, and my opinion of Him never changes His faithfulness, thankfully.

Fast forward to early January 2018, 14 months post Army discharge. I was home sick in bed with a bad cold. I gathered my calendar and a notebook and began thinking about my goals for the year. Vaguely, I knew I wanted to offer more of myself to the people around me. Not fitness inspiration or healthy recipes or more cute pictures of my dogs (those are all right up my comfortable alley, by the way), but something really and truly me. Something that would help people in the deepest sense of the word. I scribbled a few words down in my notebook. Transparency. Authenticity. Truth. Encouragement. A vision started to form in my mind. I thought about my own gifts – faith, working with my hands and writing. Writing had gone by the wayside ever since I started having vertigo in 2013, and I missed it like an old friend.

Kristin Armstrong is one of my favorite writers, and she truly speaks to my soul. In her book, Work in Progress: An Unfinished Woman's Guide to Grace, she addresses the delicate topic of motherhood. She says that all women were created to be a mother, but not necessarily in the traditional, physical way. She writes that all women have the ability to give life to something deep in our souls – a ministry, a business, a work of art, music, or actual children. We have the capacity to nurture and sustain, and there is where we find our hearts.

Since 2013 I have felt the labor pains of bringing a book into the world. I could feel its life growing inside, waiting for the perfect conditions to fully manifest. Something deep in was designed to give life to written words. It is my calling and my passion. Over the years, God has spoken things into my heart, slowly bringing the vision into focus. Just a month before I became ill in 2013, I wrote this:

Several weeks ago, I felt God speak to me, that writing is a gift He has given me, and I need to use it more. I love the movie Chariots of

Fire. Eric Liddell is a runner and a missionary, pressured by people in each field to choose either runner or serving the Lord. He explains to his sister, who thinks his running is nonsense, that running is so much more than just running:

"I believe God made me for a purpose, but He also made me fast. And when I run I feel His pleasure. To win is to honor Him."

For me, to not write would do God a disservice. Not because I have some great talent or a novel message, but because He has placed this love in my heart, *and it is through writing that He speaks to me and wants me share with others. When I write, I see things clearer, and God shows me little details and nuances that I missed the first time around. It is a way of learning, internalizing and making sense of His voice. Like it was for Eric, I don't distinguish my writing from ministry.*

But, like any seasoned procrastinator, I put it off and ignored the tug to write, and made plenty of excuses. After all, why did my story matter? Who am I to think people want to read about *me*? *No one wants to see the mess and hurt inside me*, I thought.

Yet, something else overpowered the voice that told me to stop before I even began. I knew the more transparent I was with my battles, the more it gives permission for other people to share their own struggles. People crave authenticity and meaningful connection in a world filled with carefully manufactured reality. I decided the only way I could offer something truly valuable and *real* to people was to use my gift and share my heart – the struggle and the devastation and the growth and the blessings – all of it.

I hadn't been able to find any post-Army employment and had a vague inclination that maybe God was intentionally closing the doors of the 22 jobs I had applied for. So, there in bed, surrounded by piles of Kleenex and stacks of half-read books, I took a deep breath and asked God what He wanted from me. I felt His gentle voice tell me now was the time to write.

I immediately texted my decision to Deborah McLain, one of the co-founders of Creative Force Press, and my friend of 13 years, Ann. I knew that once I made my intentions known, there was no turning back. No more excuses. Neither one of them was going to let me off the hook. It was terrifying and exhilarating. I also understood if God was for me in this endeavour, He would give me the means to accomplish it. How it would all happen was obscure, so I simply trusted He would give me the strength and clarity to tell my story.

I emailed the news to my maternal grandma, Dolly, who is a prolific writer and authored her first book at age 91. She has kept journals every day for over 40 years, and even at age 97 is asked to speak in churches and on radio programs. God speaks to her every day, and she turns those words into beautiful poetry. Every holiday or family gathering she writes an anecdote to share or recounts stories from a bygone era, like when she was a new bride to my grandfather, a freshly minted Army Air Corps pilot. She called me later that day, her voice choky with tears.

"Meredith Anne, I've been praying that God would remind you that you've got a book in you, child! I'm glad to see he's finally gotten through to you!" she finished with a laugh.

I knew writing this book would be the challenge of my lifetime, and I was apprehensive about digging back into the past – the ugliness, the hurt, the darkness, and other memories I'd rather not revive. I was afraid some of those really devastating and inferior feelings would creep back in and somehow take me captive again. Our past has a sneaky way of doing that sometimes. But as I wrote, I felt God pouring out grace upon grace, as if He'd dropped a wall between me and the past. And I knew it wouldn't hurt me again. Even as I waded into the murkiest waters, I knew God was overseeing every step. He gave me eyes to see the past for what it was – broken and irreversible – but also eyes to see His unwavering goodness to me. As I wrote, new lessons and joys popped up, reminding me that God is *always* redeeming our brokenness for His glory.

One of the most beautiful symbols of God's faithfulness is in the Old Testament, when the Israelites would put down stone markers as a visual and lasting reminder of the goodness of God. At one point, the outnumbered Israelites faced an army of angry Philistines, which they had no chance of defeating on their own. God threw the Philistines into confusion, and the Israelite warriors defeated their enemies. Afterwards Samuel, a man of God, built a memorial.

From 1 Samuel 7:12 – *Samuel then took a large stone and placed it between the towns of Mizpah and Jeshanah. He named it Ebenezer (which means "the stone of help"), for he said, "Up to this point the LORD has helped us!"*

This book is my Ebenezer stone, my testimony of God's immense faithfulness to me, even when His face was shrouded with clouds. Even during the seasons of my life when there was no apparent lesson or grand revelation, no prize for the trial, no understanding in retrospection. During every graceless season, He stood like a mountain behind the clouds. He stood and He still stands.

Prologue

I filed into the gym along with my high school varsity basketball teammates and our coach, matching duffels slung over our shoulders. We slid our bags behind us onto the bleachers as we settled in to watch our junior varsity team warm up before their game. I was 17 then, an average basketball player with an affinity for working hard at sports, but not so much at my schoolwork. Our team, the Bulldogs, was on the road at a small farm town much like our own. I sat next to my best friend and teammate, Kelly, like usual, and we gabbed about honors Spanish homework and the new baby calf on her farm, which she was bottle-feeding. We watched the teams go through their warm-up drills and the announcers presented the starting lineups for the game. It was business as usual for a small-town JV basketball game.

During the National Anthem, an Army ROTC color guard presented the flag, something I had never seen before. They were dressed in freshly pressed woodland camo uniforms and spit shined boots, looking disciplined and professional. Something about them was intriguing and intimidating simultaneously. I leaned over to Kelly after the music was finished and said, "That's going to be me in two years." It was a bold statement from a shy small-town girl who had never even met a real soldier before.

The closest I'd come to military life was through my maternal grandfather. My grandpa George was a decorated B-17 bomber pilot and World War II hero who retired when my mom was a young girl. I was proud of his achievements, but could never really relate on a personal level to his military career. It seemed like the war happened in a different lifetime. To me as a kid, grandpa was a quiet but strong man – a farmer, retired schoolteacher and former wrestling coach. He taught my sisters and I how to jump up and click our heels, knew the name of every living tree, bush and flower, and proudly showed us off when we visited him and my grandma Dolly in Florida at their winter home. He was a brilliant storyteller with a wicked sense of humor, and a bit of a mischief-maker. He was never Lieutenant Colonel Redden to me, just grandpa, who let us put barrettes in his hair while he napped in his recliner and walked our dog, Holly, when he came to visit. I assumed that I had inherited exactly none of his qualities. I didn't know how I could be related to someone so legendary. He was brave and charismatic. I was shy and anxious.

I spent a better part of my junior year of high school fretting over the prospect of college and figuring out what I wanted to do with my life. The weight of the world sat on my shoulders, thinking I had to have it all figured out by the time I crossed the stage at high school graduation. Plain Jane, that was me. Fully convinced that I wasn't good at anything, my lack of talent would certainly forever sentence me to a young adulthood of mediocrity. At the same time, I yearned restlessly for something more, outside the cornfield confines of my hometown of Mahomet, Illinois, population 4,400.

Memories blur together of the many nights sitting at the kitchen counter with my parents during that year, talking through college options, in tears or near tears at the prospect of choosing a major and a school to attend. My grades up to that point had been respectable, but universities weren't going to throw academic scholarships my way.

As a child, seeing the future as an opportunity for adventure wasn't typical, but rather a scary void to be cautiously navigated. In my mind, there was no room for trial and error, for making mistakes or taking chances when it came to my future. There was only one focus: iron out every possible hitch in the way ahead. The unfamiliar terrified me. Spontaneity was not a word in my vocabulary. So, there I sat at that Formica kitchen table under a long fluorescent light, endlessly trying to think of just *one thing* that I wouldn't mind studying and then doing for the rest of my life. It seemed impossible.

Once, when I was a teenager, my mom told me that as a young child I was *terrified of life*. The statement isn't too far from the truth. I can vividly remember my first day of preschool, walking inside the unfamiliar building clutching my dad's hand, a pink plastic My Little Pony tight in my other hand. Refusing to make eye contact with my new teachers or the other kids, I stared self-consciously at the brightly patterned rug while my dad spoke with my teachers and gently tried to coax me into a few words. My terror at this new environment brought out a stubborn streak a mile wide. From that day on, I refused to participate in any activities in my new preschool, with the bizarre exception of singing a solo in a kiddie circus production we performed at the end of the year. I'd sing and dance in front of an audience all day long, but heaven forbid you ask me to make chocolate space ice cream in a Ziploc bag with the rest of the class. It wasn't going to happen.

My mom, bless her heart, earnestly tried to facilitate my college selection process. Despite our molasses-in-January-slow dial-up Internet and dinosaur of a desktop computer, she would diligently, albeit slowly, research universities and areas of study online to help show me different options and opportunities. I considered marine biology, linguistics and (briefly) fashion design as potential career paths. Despite my shyness and disbelief in my own skills, I had within me some wild idealistic inclinations. I wanted to save the disenfranchised people of the world. I pictured myself in some savage jungle, rendering medical aid to a remote Amazon tribe, or translating Spanish for a missionary organization deep in Mexico, or maybe even singing on Broadway. For a girl who couldn't even work up the nerve to talk to an adult on the telephone, these fantasies were an extremely far stretch.

After many frustrating and tearful conversations about the future, I solidly decided I was going to be a nurse. It sounded attainably heroic. I was smart enough to handle the coursework and I assumed it would be a good outlet for my compassionate heart. Actually, I thought it was the only career option for someone like me who really cared about meeting the needs of people. I was 17 and didn't exactly have a broad view of the world from my quiet hometown.

While looking into respectable nursing programs for me, my mom stumbled across information about the Reserve Officer Training Corps, or ROTC, which allowed students to concurrently study and train to become a military officer. They would pay for my school, and I would give the military four years afterwards. As scary as it sounded, it also fell right in line with my idealistic search for adventure and doing something non-standard with my life. Shortly after that day, in a rare fit of boldness, I mentally committed to becoming an Army nurse.

That winter and spring I applied to only three colleges, all within a few hours' drive of home. Anything farther away from that was out of the question. I received an acceptance letter from all three, but one in particular offered me a four-year, all expenses paid ROTC scholarship. They also had a great nursing program, according to my guidance counselor, Mrs. Warren. Without feeling the need to put much thought into the decision, I decided I was going to attend Olivet Nazarene University in Bourbonnais, Illinois. It was a small private Christian school, only 90 minutes from home. It felt like a safe, nurturing option. Making the decision and knowing the next four years of my life were already planned out and paid for felt really, really good to my anxious young adult self. I liked plans in the same way that I liked recipes and lists – they gave me a sense of purpose and told me what to do next.

With an acceptance letter, a full-ride scholarship and a clean bill of health from the Department of Defense in my hand, my future looked smooth before me. I was scared to death of the unknowns, but the path I had started to walk felt right. My family and friends were surprised by my declared career path, but proud nonetheless. And for the first time in my young life, I felt like I had something akin to vision. God seemed to give me a tangible, attainable dream in my heart, and it was truly powerful. I could see a crack in the door to the bigger world outside of my otherwise lovingly sheltered childhood. Adulthood lay before me – a life with responsibilities, purpose and challenges.

Shortly before high school graduation, my grandma Dolly gave me a copy of Oswald Chambers' book, *My Utmost for His Highest*. She loved that book dearly and gave each of my three sisters and I a copy at various times in our lives. That summer, amidst a family road trip and college preparation, I began reading the daily devotionals from time to time. One particular reading from July 6 stood out to me, titled *Visions Becoming Reality*. I read the black script in the small turquoise book twice through, marking the verse at the top of the page with a blue ink pen. *"The parched ground shall become a pool[1],"* it read. And underneath, *"God gives us a vision, and then He takes us down to the valley to batter us into the shape of that vision. God has to take us into the valley and put us through fires and floods to batter us into shape, until we get to the point where he can trust us with the reality of the vision."*

I knew without a doubt God had given me a small, fragile

---

[1] Isaiah 35:7

vision of becoming an Army officer a little more than a year prior. At the time I didn't fully understand the weight of what He was leading me to, but I trusted His call on my life and knew He would equip me to handle the responsibility of it. I would spend the next four years at college, simultaneously earning a degree and training to be an officer, working towards the *reality of the vision*. Eventually, on graduation day, I would earn my commission in the Army and begin the greatest adventure of my life.

CHAPTER 1

The Shape of the Vision

May 5, 2008, I stood in front of my graduating class at Olivet Nazarene University, shoulder to shoulder with six of my peers, each of us in our crisp Army green dress uniforms and black berets. We raised our right hands and took an oath, swearing to support and defend the Constitution of the United States, officially becoming Army Second Lieutenants. Later that afternoon, in a ceremony with friends and family, we pinned on shiny gold bars and ate cake to celebrate. Ending one long journey and beginning a new one was exhilarating.

The four previous years had gone by in a flash, but they definitely hadn't turned out how I had expected. I arrived to campus in the fall of 2005, wide-eyed and nervous. I learned how to spit shine my black combat boots in the shared bathroom of my dorm while other girls dyed their hair or shaved their legs at the sink, looking on curiously. Each week my ROTC peers and I woke up early to run laps and do pushups on the university track long before most students stirred from their beds. Upperclassmen patiently mentored me, and I learned how to fire a weapon, make a shelter out of a poncho and follow orders.

Nursing coursework was moderately challenging, but not particularly interesting, and I hated our weekly clinicals at the local nursing home. But I plugged away, running from training to classes to study time, with little in between. In the evenings my protective roommate, Becca, would patrol the floor of our dorm, quieting anyone with turned-up music and diverting loud conversations behind closed doors so that I could get adequate sleep before my 5:15 a.m. alarm. I saw my family at least once a month when my dad would pick me up Friday afternoons for a weekend at home and drop me off at the station to catch the Sunday evening train back. With no car, few friends and little free time, university life was small and contained, if not a little lonely. Summertime at home passed as quickly as the school year, and before I knew it I was headed back to campus.

I returned to Olivet for my second year feeling like a seasoned cadet, but less than thrilled about classes. Nursing school was still as odious as ever, but I pushed forward, pulling a solid B minus GPA first semester despite a total lack of attention to my studies. Clinicals at the nursing home were even more miserable, and the coursework painful. But, I was proud to tell people that I was studying to be a nurse. The title sounded great, even if I didn't relish the path it took to get there. I mentored first-year cadets, recognizing the looks of fear and confusion in their faces, which I had similarly worn the year before. My life was still small, but not quite as lonely. I had a car, given to me at the request of my paternal grandpa, who passed away that summer from cancer. A car meant increased freedom. I could drive myself home when I wanted, and I made a few more friends.

I met a scrappy red-headed nursing student named Ann, and we quickly became best friends after first making up my mind not to like her. She showed up to ROTC orientation at the beginning of the school year and I immediately rolled my eyes at her long, curled hair and denim miniskirt. She looked too pretty and fragile for the Army and thought *there is no way she will hang with the training*. The next morning she proved me wrong, running two miles of the Army Physical Fitness Test faster than every other woman and most of the men there. Over the course of a semester she became the chocolate to my vanilla, balancing my reserved timidity with her take-no-prisoners attitude. Ann the redhead suffered no fools and worked harder than anyone I had met in my life. I loved her single-mindedness and courage, and most of all, her fierce loyalty. Life had cut her no breaks, estranged her from her abusive parents at a young age. But, despite the hurt and struggle she had witnessed in her young years, she was as tough as nails and more determined than anyone to succeed at school and ROTC.

Toward the end of the school year, I suddenly realized my heart was not in my nursing studies, and I begged my parents to let me change my major to study photography. A tense few weeks followed as I tried to explain my decision to my family and professors. The Army took away my ROTC scholarship, since I had signed a contract pledging to serve the military as a nurse and threatened to make me enlist for doing so. My parents scrambled to secure grants and loans to cover the cost of tuition I had now burdened our family with. But, thanks to the particular grace of the registrar's office and some schedule reshuffling, I was able to drop most of my nursing classes. The cadre in the ROTC department scolded and lectured and threatened, but their arguments fell on deaf ears. I had made up my mind. I would cram two years' worth of art classes into the following two years, somehow.

Junior year brought a wave of new challenges. Photography and art classes were a welcome joy, but I had a lot of missed time to make up for and took on heavy course loads to make sure I could earn my degree in four semesters' time. I was not naturally talented at photography like I had hoped, but I enjoyed learning how to develop darkroom prints and shoot with different kinds of cameras. ROTC was especially hectic, as our third year was when all cadets take on new leadership roles every week and get constantly evaluated in preparation for a five-week summer assessment course, mandatory for all rising fourth year cadets. Miraculously, I earned a new scholarship covering tuition for the final three semesters of school.

Between school and a manic ROTC schedule, there was little time to slow down. I had injured my back the summer before returning to school, and it bothered me daily for months to the point where I didn't know if I was going to be able to commission into the Army. I could barely sit in a chair for more than 30 minutes and wearing a rucksack and doing physical training were out of the question. The head professor of military science at the school thought I had lost my fire to be an officer and was fishing for excuses not to commission.

God, I need Your healing and direction. Are You taking my life off the course I've on for the last three years? I couldn't continue the rigorous training I was used to with my injury, but I didn't want to get the boot and not commission. Besides the Army, there was no back up plan. Then one day in late spring I felt God gently say *I Am* to me. Moses once asked God for His name, and God simply responded with *I Am who I Am.* Suddenly, it didn't matter if I was healed, if I became an Army officer, if I knew exactly where I was going. God was enough. Because He *is,* because He existed, because every mystery of the vast universe was wrapped up in those two words, *I Am,* that could be enough for me.

Shortly after that day, my medical case was sent up to the Department of Defense Medical Review Board, which made the final determination about my condition. They approved me to continue and not long afterwards my back fully healed, just in time to fly out to Fort Lewis, Washington, for the assessment course.

⛰

Five weeks in the Evergreen State passed in a blur of rain, wet boots and constant shivering against the unseasonable cold. Even though it was June, overnight temperatures dipped into the upper 30's, and it rained almost continually, straight through the first eight out of ten days spent patrolling in the woods. We slept in Gore-Tex sacks in the bear-infested woods, exposed to the elements and swarms of bloodthirsty mosquitoes. The sacks barely kept out the steady torrent of rain and did little to keep us warm. Our cadre had forbidden us to take sleeping bags with us, believing that it wasn't going to be cold and that they would only take up valuable space in our rucksacks.

Finally, on the second to last day of patrolling, the sun broke through and burned off thick layers of clouds, warming the air and exposing, for the first time, a spectacular view of Mt. Rainier. The sunlight had a magical effect on the landscape, illuminating the golden knee-high grass and setting the scattered yellow Scotch broom bushes ablaze against the bright blue sky as we trudged past in sodden boots. The mountain was snowcapped and loomed high over the rest of the Cascade Range, making it look much bigger than its 14,000 feet. I couldn't look away – it was mesmerizing.

At the end of the course we received our evaluations from platoon cadre. As expected, they told me I was too quiet and gentle to be a good leader. Officers needed to be alphas. I needed to be loud and out front if anyone was going to take me seriously as a leader. Even my own squad of all men had ranked me last in peer evaluations for being quiet. I had heard the same lines over and over again in ROTC. *If you want anyone to take you seriously you need to be aggressive and loud.* Inwardly I rolled my eyes. My platoon mates had one-upped each other in a constant and predictable display of military pageantry for the past five weeks, vying for the spotlight and a good rating. I hated the game playing. In the real Army no one was going to care if you got the Recondo award in cadet training camp.

The one thing that ate at me the most was not the misunderstanding of my capabilities, but that in my counseling the cadre told me I was a *distraction*. That somehow my femaleness was a detractor from what the men, the real soldiers, were trying to accomplish. My blonde hair wouldn't fly in the real Army, they said. It was my first (and certainly not last) taste of the Army's deep-rooted culture of sexism.

﹏

The final year of college passed by in a blur of photography classes and ROTC training. I was itchy and restless to finally figure out my first assignment and get Army life started. Having dropped out of nursing school, my branch was still up in the air. We were required to rank our desired branches for consideration by Human Resources Command. They considered our GPA, performance at the assessment camp and various other factors. I wanted to be as close to the action as I could be, so I requested the Engineering branch, followed by Military Police as a second choice. There weren't a lot of women in either branch and they sounded a lot more fun than working in HR or the Chemical Corps.

Finally, at the beginning of our final semester, the fourth-year cadets received their assignments via a phone call from Major Creek, one of the head ROTC instructors.

"Cadet Morris, you are assigned to the Transportation Corps," he said matter-of-factly. I paused for several seconds to take in the news.

"Sir, are you kidding?" I asked. I thought he was joking. I ranked transportation near the bottom of my list. Army logistics was a pretty thankless career field, and definitely didn't seem remotely interesting.

He affirmed before concluding the conversation. There wasn't much he could say to convince me I had gotten a good assignment, and he knew it. I cried after hanging up the phone, feeling bitterly wounded for several days. *Transportation sucks.* It was about as unsexy as military jobs came. I wanted to blaze a trail and play with explosives and lead troops into combat. Any chance of that was shattered – I would be supervising truck drivers and mechanics.

Several days later I received an email saying I was assigned to Fort Lewis, my third choice of duty station after Hawaii and Colorado. I remembered back to the mountain and the fragrant, tall evergreens from the previous summer. The beauty had captivated me. *I could like it there.* My temporary duty orders also arrived, sending me to Fort Lewis for almost three months prior to mandatory new officer and transportation training. The assignment required me to help out at the five-week assessment course I had attended the previous summer. It also meant that I would step into the active duty ranks two short weeks after graduation.

Just days after commissioning, I loaded up everything I owned into my old Buick and headed west, bound for my new life as an Army officer. To say I was nervous was an understatement. There was so much about Army and military life that I didn't have a clue about. I knew how to be a leader, but that's about where my practical skills ended. My life up to that point had been relatively sheltered. I had grown up and gone to school surrounded by people who looked like me, talked like me, believed the same things that I did and did little to challenge my worldview. I possessed nothing resembling street smarts and lived under the assumption that if I worked hard and treated people kindly, they would do the same for me. Everyone was good in my eyes.

My parents prayed for me and shed a few tears as I set off, and I did my best to put on a strong front, feigning confidence. Everything we would really need to know about the Army we would learn at our first units, our cadre told us. Until then, we would rely on our leadership abilities and a lot of humility. Deep down I was chomping at the bit to finally start living out the vision I had been given years before. My passion was tempered with the exhilaration of the unknown, a constant knowing wondering if I would be *enough*, or if it would all be too much for me. I was as green as they came – eager, yet scared, bold, yet uncertain.

My stiff new uniforms packed into plastic bins in my trunk looked foreign to me with the unfamiliar unit patch and new lieutenant rank on them. My freshly shaped beret looked hardly worn, and my new desert boots were much too clean. I felt like a kid playing dress up in a soldier's uniform. It hadn't hit me yet that I was an officer. Everything felt surreal as I drove the endless stretch of I-90 West, watching the plains turn to mountains.

△△

The next seven months were hectic as I got my feet underneath me. I still didn't feel like I was in the real Army, spending most of my time surrounded by my peers, most as inexperienced as me. I wanted to get through all of the mandatory training as quickly as possible so I could finally get to my first unit. After a spectacular and exhausting summer working 18-hour days at Fort Lewis training cadets, I moved on to Fort Sill, Oklahoma for new lieutenant training. I battled a six-week case of mono in the oppressive heat, refusing to stop training, fearing that I would have to take the course over again. Even after spending the day outside in triple digit temperatures, I would return to the barracks and take scalding hot showers until the hot water ran out, unable to get warm. In the evenings I would be fast asleep in my bunk by 7:30 p.m., only to wake up in the middle of the night with sweat-soaked sheets and a sickening pain underneath my shoulder blades.

The cadre had pity on me towards the end of the course, allowing me to sleep through several days of field training. From the cocoon of my sleeping bag I listened to the rest of my company react to a simulated artillery attack and mass casualty drill on the mock Forward Operating Base and was grateful for the excuse to not have to participate in the circus. Extreme fatigue overtook my body and I slept through the day and well into the night, almost an 18-hour stretch. Our company ended our final week in the field with a middle of the night ten-mile road march. It was mandatory for graduating the course, so I hauled my wrecked body out of bed and completed the march, barely putting one foot in front of the other until the drudgery was over.

The final stretch of my officer training took place at Fort Eustis, Virginia, where all Army Transportation officers receive their schooling. I doubt that anyone learned much about Army logistics at the three-month course. It still felt like we were playing Army and few lieutenants in our 60-person class seemed to be taking the meager course material seriously. My friend Molly, who I met earlier in the summer at Fort Lewis, showed me around her home state on the weekends. We had weekly chocolate chip pancake dinners and watched new episodes of The Office and ventured to Charlottesville or historic sites on the weekends. The course offered endless opportunities for leisure and social activities, which we took full advantage of. Still, at the end of the course shortly before Christmas, I was eager to get on the road and report to my unit in Fort Lewis.

▲▲▲

Once again, I found myself on the long stretch of I-90, driving through desolate winter landscapes heading westward. I had traded in my old Buick for a new Jeep at my dad's urging before heading out on the long drive back to Washington. Still, everything I owned fit easily into the back of my vehicle. After seven months of itinerant living, I was ready to be in one place for a while. Hotel and barracks living got old quickly.

Late in the evening of January 2, 2009, I finally arrived at Fort Lewis again. Heavy, wet flakes of snow began to fall as I arrived at the in-processing building, covering the parking lot with a thick carpet of slush. Even in the dead of the winter it was just as captivating as I had remembered. I breathed a sigh of resolute relief as I walked inside. I was finally here, and it was time to get to work.

Chapter 2

Drinking from a Firehose

I reported to my new unit, the Brigade Support Battalion (BSB), mid-January, just as they were ramping up to leave in three weeks for a month-long rotation at the National Training Center in Fort Irwin, California as part of a larger 4,000-Soldier Stryker brigade. The BSB was responsible for all the medical and logistical services for the entire unit, which was slated to go to Afghanistan for a year, beginning that summer. I arrived right at the peak of their training cycle. The trip to NTC would mimic deployment conditions and test the readiness of the brigade. By Independence Day we would all be on a plane headed to a combat zone. The BSB assigned me to A Company, the 140-person distribution unit that was responsible for all the transportation assets, ammunition, fuel, and supply parts for the brigade. They moved a million miles an hour to keep the brigade moving forward.

The A Company commander, Captain Andrews, wasted no time in assimilating me into the pace of his busy unit. All the platoon leader positions, standard for new 2nd Lieutenants, were filled when I arrived, so I was thrown into the Executive Officer job, which felt light years above my experience level. Being XO meant I was second in command to Capt. Andrews and bore the responsibility of doing all the never-ending work of an administrative assistant getting 140 people and their equipment ready to go to war. The duties entailed everything from Human Resources to equipment accountability and making never-ending PowerPoint presentations and Excel spreadsheets for meetings. The Commander frequently went into violent fits over the documents if so much as the text font size didn't suit his fancy. Sometimes I would spend hours revising memo after memo, only for him to find some new mistake with it. The recycling bin under my desk overflowed with his discarded edits.

By the end of the first week I was exhausted and felt way in over my head. In the Army, we call the steep learning curves *drinking out of a firehose*. The phrase perfectly captured the frustration futility of jumping into an advanced position right before a deployment. Getting my feet underneath me seemed like an impossible feat. Capt. Andrews was a demanding perfectionist and lead with the philosophy that praise and affirmation makes weak leaders. Heavy-handed criticism was the order of the day under his command, and he doled it out in generous amounts, especially to his subordinate officers. I was still as green as could be and knew relatively little about practical logistics or what was required of the XO position. His senior enlisted adviser, First Sergeant Gregory, was outwardly good tempered, but underneath his smiling façade there was a deep well of favoritism and mockery and a deep dislike of officers.

Consequently, the Soldiers of A Company were worn out and disgruntled, having maintained a near constant schedule of supporting field training exercises in Yakima for months on end under toxic command. They wistfully longed to be deployed; deployed so that life could *slow down*. Most of them would be parsed out to various Logistics Support Teams during the deployment, supporting infantry and cavalry battalions far away from the A Company headquarters. I envied the other lieutenants in the company who got to lead the LSTs and escape the scrutiny of the unit's leadership. John, Matt and Emil were all 30-something men who had been enlisted in the Army prior to becoming officers. Their experience made them cynical towards the current state of the company. They, too, were counting down the days until they could get away from Capt. Andrews and his domineering ways.

The month at NTC with the brigade was a miserable nightmare, filled with sleepless nights and barely controlled chaos. Capt. Andrews was not only demanding, but also controlling, as I found out. He didn't trust anyone, and constantly micromanaged his subordinates. Anyone who failed to meet his absurd standards faced harsh criticism. He forced me to stay awake until long after midnight in our company's TOC[2] on principle, not because there was work to be done, and allowed me no more than a few hours of sleep each night. He and 1st Sgt. Gregory would laugh and ridicule me as I nodded off into my hands at my computer during the day, barely able to function. They nicknamed me Creampuff and told me I was weak and pathetic. 1st Sgt. Gregory crafted a paper nametag for me with *Lt. Creampuff* written on it, sticking it to my uniform with duct tape, much to my shame.

I did my best to play along with the jokes, not wanting to make waves in my new unit or seem insubordinate. I was still very much naïve to the Army culture and figured their constant ridicule was a form of hazing for new lieutenants. I reeked of insecurity and innocence and was an easy target for their abuse. Prior to joining the Army, I had never really found myself in a situation where I needed to stand up for myself, and now floundered at the opportunity to finally do so.

Fortunately, the manic pace of NTC made the month go by relatively quickly. I finally felt like I was starting to gain some traction and understand how the unit worked to a greater extent. My knowledge still had some massive blind spots, but I was learning. My family and friends kept me afloat by sending care packages and letters. There was even a small heart-shaped box of candy and a singing card from my parents for Valentine's Day.

The BSB practiced running logistical convoys and reacting to enemy contact. I spent most of my time in the company command post, doing my best to track the real time status of each person, vehicle and piece of company equipment across multiple locations at NTC. Occasionally, our progress would be interrupted by a simulated mortar attack, sending the A Company headquarters into a frenzy to get accountability of all of their 140 Soldiers. Capt. Andrews demanded that we be the first company in the battalion to get full accountability of all their soldiers during each drill and came down hard on me if the entire process took more than a couple minutes. He did very little work himself, instead preferring to sit at a table in the command post and catch his soldiers underperforming without offering any real teachable

---

[2] Tactical Operation Center, a military headquarters area

moments. It was micromanaging in its most destructive form.

⛰

After we returned to Fort Lewis, the real work began of packing up all the unit's equipment and preparing it to get shipped overseas for the deployment via train, boat and trucks. Capt. Andrews put me in charge of the task of overseeing the entire load-up process. Some days we stayed at work until well after midnight, packing and inventorying and repacking containers until they were up to standard. I practically lived at the rail yard for a week, making sure every truck and trailer and container was correctly processed and marked for shipment. It was particularly miserable but kept me out of the office and away from the commander, who still managed to call my cell phone demanding an update if he hadn't heard from me in more than an hour or two.

As the intensity of A Company's preparation increased, so did Capt. Andrews' anxiety about the upcoming deployment. His anger frequently found its target on me. He had delegated nearly all of his responsibilities to me, and at the slightest sign of imperfection or uncertainty would raise his voice at me, often in front of soldiers. His face would turn bright red and his upper lip twitched as he berated me over an incorrect PowerPoint slide or someone in the company dropping the ball on a task. Every minute appearance of failure within the unit was my fault and every success was because of his superior leadership. More than once I found myself on his office floor doing pushups for substandard performance.

Not long after our return from NTC, Capt. Andrews' abuse took a sinister turn. One weekend while his wife was away with their kids visiting family, he lured me into his home after a basketball game with A Company under the pretense of showing me around. He took advantage of me, pushing me down on the couch in his living room, surrounded by portraits of his smiling wife and kids as I tried feebly to crawl away and push his 230-pound frame off of me. I was confused and terrified, unable to make sense of what was happening. I felt powerless to stand up for myself against him, and ashamed that I had brought his inappropriate attention onto myself.

My insecurity and lack of know-how proved an easy target for his predatory abuse. My humble, small-town upbringing and Christian college education had protected me from the cruel realities of a broken world. I blindly trusted people, naively assuming the best about them, never realizing that anyone would or could ever try to hurt me. My faith in myself and belief in God were toppled in an instant that day. There wasn't grace enough to cover my shameful mistake, I thought. Why hadn't my trust in God been enough to protect me from walking into a terrible situation like this? Good Christian girls like me didn't find themselves in my position. It wasn't Capt. Andrews' fault – I truly believed *I* was the one who had let it happen. And so my deep shame kept me in darkness. I didn't tell anyone what had happened out of fear that it would end my career, and the deep-rooted belief that what had happened was entirely my fault. I carried the burden with me every moment of every day.

Still, outwardly to Lt. Col. Jefferson and the rest of the battalion staff Capt. Andrews was a charismatic favorite. He could go from cutting his leaders down in the motor pool to laughing and joking with the other commanders in a matter of minutes, with no one the wiser. He was the shining star of the battalion yet his stretched-thin company, heading straight for burnout, struggled to keep up with his constant circus of absurd demands.

His various forms of abuse towards me escalated severely leading up to our summer deployment. But despite his gross mistreatment I couldn't see how deeply Capt. Andrews had manipulated me. He always told me he was harder on me than anyone else because he truly cared about me and wanted to make me a great leader. He never broke down the other lieutenants like he did me, and I suspected it was because they were men. The more he crushed me, the more desperate I became to please him. I craved his approval, and became a submissive, beat-down shell of myself by the time we left for Afghanistan. He terrified me and put my guts in constant knots, but soon I wanted nothing more than a drop of praise from his lips.

As June came to a close the brigade was finally ready to leave for Afghanistan. Up until that point I hadn't had time to really think about the implications of the deployment or what it would really mean for A Company. We owned all the transportation assets in the brigade and would be running logistical resupply convoys to all corners of Kandahar, Helmand and Zabul Provinces. Each battalion and company were going to be parceled out to different outposts to cover a much larger operating area than it was equipped to handle. A Company, located centrally at Kandahar Airfield would make sure they stayed supplied with ammunition, food and fuel.

Few of the brigade's leaders knew much about Afghanistan. They had been preparing for nearly a year for a deployment to Iraq, only to find out five months prior to leaving that the unit would be going to Afghanistan. The news blindsided the brigade and sent them scrambling to adjust their training. By mid-2009 Operation Enduring Freedom[3] was intensifying, eventually leading President Obama to call for an American troop surge at the urging of General Stanley McChrystal, the commander of coalition forces in Afghanistan. The southern provinces of Kandahar and Helmand Provinces were deadly Taliban nests, littered with roadside IED[4]s and plagued with intense fighting, and we would meet them head on.

Shortly before we left, A Company received a new 2nd Lieutenant named Andy. He had just finished transportation officer training and would be heading downrange with us. Andy had been a Staff Sergeant in a Ranger regiment prior to becoming an officer. He was an unbending, chain-smoking, profanity factory of a 30-something man who loved going toe-to-toe with Capt. Andrews. His audacity to pick fights with a superior officer stupefied me on a daily basis. Andy would brush off the commander's threats and say, "What are they gonna do to us, Morris? Make us second lieutenants and send us to Afghanistan?"

The chain of flights into Afghanistan put me into a time-warped

---

[3] 2001-2014 U.S. counterterrorism efforts in Afghanistan, Philippines and Africa

[4] Improvised Explosive Device

haze of sunrises and sunsets as we flew eastward over the Atlantic, stopping in Indianapolis, Canada, Iceland, Germany, Romania, Turkey, and finally Kyrgyzstan. The chartered Ryan Air plane was heavy laden with a full manifest of soldiers and their equipment. It could only handle a few hours of flying before the pilot was required to touch down to refuel for an hour or so. We reached Manas Airbase in Kyrgyzstan three days after we left Washington, foggy headed and cramped from sitting for hours on end with little legroom. Our flight group stayed on the U.S. Air Force base for two days, enjoying what we thought might be our last hours with flushing toilets and running water for a long time, sleeping on metal bunks in gymnasium-sized tents. At breakfast on our last morning we learned of Michael Jackson's death from the muted TVs on the dining facility walls. Watching American news channels from several thousand miles away on the way to a combat zone was surreal.

Nearing midnight we crammed ourselves into an Air Force C-17 aircraft for the flight into Kandahar Airfield, better known as KAF. Next to me, the A Company personnel clerk, a young woman named Sergeant Michaels, settled in for the two-hour trip. The plane had airline-type seats installed six-wide on pallets in the main cargo area. There was barely enough room between rows for even an average-sized person to sit comfortably. The crew required us to don our body armor for the flight, making the squeeze into the seats even more uncomfortable. Once we sat down there was no getting up until the plane landed. Finally, after all the cargo was loaded in behind us, we ascended into the warm night sky. As we neared the airspace over Afghanistan the flight crew shut the interior lights off, save for a couple dim tactical red bulbs high inside the belly of the plane. We donned our helmets for the final descent then plunged steeply into the darkness.

Chapter 3

Sea of Sharks

We arrived at KAF to very little. The southern area of the base where the brigade was assigned to set up shop was an expansive wasteland of shin deep moon dust. The soft talcum powder-fine sand kicked up into swirling brown clouds with the slightest provocation. Every surface, indoors and outside, was covered with a fine layer of the dust, which clogged air filters, jammed weapons and irritated our lungs. Nothing clean, including us, stayed clean for very long. The temperatures in Kandahar were easily in the triple digits in the heat of the day. Industrial air conditioner units in the sleeping tents struggled to keep a comfortable temperature when the sun rose high in the sky. Stepping outside felt like opening a hot oven door – the heat was so intense it hurt your skin. Bottled water left exposed to the sunlight would scald your tongue and was warm enough to steep tea in. The whole base smelled strongly of raw waste. Large, open sewage tanks, known by KAF residents as the Poo Pond, made the air thick with the smell of sulphur at all hours of the day and night.

The only telephone or Internet we had access to were in a small wooden building a half-mile walk from our headquarters. The building, which reeked of cigarette smoke and body odor, was run by civilians and provided connectivity to all the coalition forces on the southern side of KAF. Often, the wait to call home or check email was upwards of 90 minutes. It was almost easier to not call home at all. Most of us purchased cheap Nokia cell phones and loaded Roshan calling card minutes on to them. Cell signal was hit or miss and all our calls were monitored, but we could occasionally call home for a few minutes to check in.

Soldiers slept 20 people to a tent, stacked closely on top of each other on 10 sets of metal bunk beds with cheap metal spring mattresses.

My only concession as an officer was getting a bottom bunk near the door so that I could be easily awakened when someone needed me in the middle of the night. Portable toilets and water piped to a tent outfitted with a rig of showerheads sufficed for a bathroom. The accommodations were cramped and sparse and offered no protection from the frequent barrages of incoming mortars, but they were an adequate refuge. In the company female tent we crafted small amounts of privacy, stringing up ponchos and blankets between our bunks.

We spent the first month in country getting settled and ready to run operations, receiving our vehicles and equipment and pushing out the LSTs to their sites. Somehow, we managed to conquer the dust bowl on KAF, thanks largely in part to several tons of gravel. Soldiers from the company constructed a beautiful command post out of plywood and two by four planks, complete with a front porch and tin roof. Through layers of chain link fence and coiled concertina wire, we had an uninterrupted view of the desert sunset, which provided a stunning backdrop to Tarnak Farms, a former al Qaeda training camp just a few hundred yards away.

Sgt. Michaels was my right-hand woman, and together we established processes and procedures to keep the heartbeat of the company running. Even with very little equipment and no phone or computer connections we found a way to scrap together resources to provide for the A Company Soldiers and track our incoming equipment. She was a cheerful, eager worker and I was grateful to have a teammate working by my side in the command post to share the load.

Andy, despite his abrasiveness, quickly became my only friend, offering mentorship and encouragement on days when Capt. Andrews was particularly heinous and unreasonable. John, Matt and Emil had long left for other bases with their teams, which left Andy and I as the only two lieutenants in the company at the headquarters. Capt. Andrews forbid me to go anywhere on KAF alone, especially at night, so naturally Andy and I became battle buddies, going to the chow hall or gym together. The double standard of protectiveness seemed unfair and outrageous to me, but the commander had already yelled at me several times for being alone, so I obliged him.

By early August, A Company was almost fully operational. We worked seven days a week, for at least 12 hours a day, if things were slow. Most days, I was in the command post by 7:00 a.m. at the latest and returned to my tent long after dark. If there was a convoy mission, we didn't sleep until everyone returned safely. The pace was exhausting.

Capt. Andrews still held me in his tight, abusive grip, but having a friend in Andy made life more tolerable, though even he didn't fully understand the depths of the commander's dark oppression. Other Soldiers in A Company frequently asked if I was okay. Capt. Andrews had a penchant for public embarrassment, and on nearly a daily basis would scream at me outside the command post, his face red and twitching. Every minor error, whether out of my own young ignorance or by sheer accident warranted his twisted barrage of verbal and emotional abuse.

Glimmers of moments where I dared be proud of myself were quickly smothered with his furious tales of my shortcomings. Any compliments from battalion leadership were wet-blanketed back by Capt. Andrews. *He* was the only person whose compliments mattered, and conditioned me to listen to no voice, critical or praising, other than him. I lived and died by his words. No matter how hard I tried to have thick skin and let his constant criticism roll off, he had crawled too deeply under my skin for me to do so. Every tear that rolled down my cheeks under the relentless desert sun fueled his sadistic thirst for power over me and drained me of my will to live.

Sgt. Michaels, my assistant, was responsible for running our daily reports up to the battalion headquarters. Personnel accountability was due each morning by 0800, and I relied on her to close the book on the task. One morning though, the accountability report didn't make it to the HQ, sending Capt. Andrews into a fury. He hated looking irresponsible in front of BSB leadership. I assured him that Sgt. Michaels had taken care of it. I had seen her with the report in hand that morning as she left the command post, and after her return she confirmed it had been delivered. Through either a misunderstanding or neglect, Sgt. Michaels hadn't made it to the TOC to turn in the report, and I suffered the wrath of the commander for what was ultimately my irresponsibility.

Capt. Andrews wouldn't rest until all parties were punished appropriately. I hated the prospect of an ugly confrontation, but I knew I had to talk to Sgt. Michaels and figure out why she had lied to me about something as small as whether or not a report made it up to HQ. Up to that point she had been an incredibly reliable soldier, fulfilling each task above and beyond her duties.

Things got messy quickly. There was an ugly confrontation, as I anticipated, and Sgt. Michaels responded defensively, blaming me for not delivering the report. A few short hours later, Capt. Andrews pulled me aside.

"You're sleeping with Andy, aren't you?" he asked angrily, his lip starting to get its telltale quiver.

"No! I'm not!" I retorted defensively. Capt. Andrews controlled my whereabouts so carefully that he would know if there was even a five-minute window in my day where I was unaccounted for.

He went on to explain that Sgt. Michaels, angry about being accused of lying, had gone straight to 1st Sgt. Gregory to file a complaint about my behavior. She believed I had been acting unprofessional and was engaged in an inappropriate relationship with Andy. It was preposterous. He was the only other person of my rank in our unit, and I had to have a babysitter of sorts at all times. It would have been inappropriate and borderline fraternization for me to go everywhere or be seen eating every meal with an enlisted soldier. But, being seen with Andy every day led people to speculate anyway. There was no winning the battle against perception.

Capt. Andrews forbade me to go anywhere with Andy from that point forward. He didn't want me to be seen alone speaking to him or be anywhere near him. From that day on *he* would be my escort. If I needed to eat or go to the gym or do anything outside of the 50-meter radius of our headquarters, he would go with me. If he hadn't completely controlled my life by that point, he surely did after that day. Day or night, I could hardly get away from him. Andy was furious about the accusations, and pushed his boundaries, urging me to buck the commander's new rules, which only tightened Capt. Andrews' grip on me. If he ever saw me speaking to Andy, even in broad daylight in a group of soldiers he would quickly pull me aside and berate me for

34

creating an inappropriate perception.

The waters muddied even further when I found inappropriate messages between Sgt. Michaels and her husband, an infantryman in one of the battalions in our brigade, on our secure positional tracking system in our command post. The messages were visible to anyone on the system and used to communicate tactically with vehicles out on missions. I was furious about the misuse of secure government property, especially at a time when we had soldiers on the road. I verbally warned her not to do it again, despite 1st Sgt. Gregory's insistence that I let it go. Two days later I found public messages between Sgt. Michaels and her husband again. This time, they were bad-mouthing me. I was irate at her flagrant disobedience and decided to give her a written counseling statement, which is the first and tamest step in disciplining a soldier.

In a matter of days, I went under investigation for "threatening" Sgt. Michaels. I had told her that continued disobedience of her superior officers would eventually lead to the ruin of her career. I was hotheaded at the time and perhaps came across as a little scary. She took it as a dangerous threat and brought my words to the attention of the battalion Equal Opportunity officer.

The EO officer looking in to my behavior advised me to stand down any punishment that I was trying to exact. She said that everyone liked Sgt. Michaels and I was causing problems by making her disobedience into an issue. Capt. Andrews and 1st Sgt. Gregory, who had initially supported me counseling Sgt. Michaels, suddenly turned on me, saying I should have let it go, and that I could no longer pursue any discipline against her. Lt. Col. Jefferson had gotten involved, telling Capt. Andrews to do whatever it took to make all the issues I was suddenly causing to *go away*. I would soon enough find out what that meant.

Over the course of several days things in A Company got worse. My behavior suddenly took center stage and caused bad blood and dissention within the ranks. Many of the platoon sergeants, being friends with Sgt. Michaels, became embroiled in the unproductive gossip, leading to breakdowns in trust and communication. Andy and I unwittingly became the elephant in the room and heard the whispers and gossip any time we were seen together, even if it was on a mission. Coupled with the fiasco with Sgt. Michaels, things got ugly quickly, until they finally reached a breaking point.

One early morning in late August, just as dawn was starting to break, Capt. Andrews and 1st Sgt. Gregory led myself, Andy, and the platoon sergeants out to a back road along the fence separating KAF from the vast desert. We were in our physical training uniforms and carried our M4 rifles slung over our shoulders. No one was sure what was happening or why the command team had called a leaders' meeting at 5:30 a.m.

The commander arranged us in a circle, and then broke the silence.

"As you guys know there's been a lot of bad blood and gossip lately about certain members of this company, and I don't like where things are going," he began. "I want to give everyone the opportunity to one by one get everything off your chest about Lt. Morris that you need to."

I was aghast. Respectable leaders didn't do things like this, I thought. They stood up for their subordinates and didn't drag them through the mud. Maybe I hadn't flawlessly handled myself in each situation I found myself in, but I was young and inexperienced. My 24th birthday was days away, and I had barely been in the army for over a year, yet I was responsible for leading convoys across the deadliest routes in Afghanistan. Dozens of lives were in my hands every time we went outside the wire. I took my job incredibly seriously and worked harder than any of my peers to prove it.

There in the gray morning twilight, each person present took their turn to air their grievances about my unprofessionalism and poor behavior, and how perceptions about me were causing distractions amongst their soldiers. Their attacks deeply wounded me, and I felt as if any moment someone would start throwing actual stones. I was a conscientious hard worker and had poured my heart and soul into doing right by A Company, so I thought. My desperation to be *enough* had gotten me nowhere. I had never felt so alone and despised in my entire life. I didn't know whom I could trust. I didn't even feel like I could trust my own judgment, if that very moment was where it had led me.

A deep darkness that I had struggled to keep at bay the last several months rolled in and swallowed me up, snuffing out my last flame of hope. It was terrifyingly unfamiliar and disorienting, but I resigned myself to its heaviness. A tiny, persistent voice in the back of my head told me I reaped what I sowed. If I hadn't been so weak, so easily manipulated or just *better* then I never would have been such an easy target. I deserved every minute of Capt. Andrews' warped abuse and attention. I deserved the darkness. I deserved to be a pariah. There was no light left for people like me. At that moment I was convinced God had left me to destruction. How could he possibly love someone so irreversibly wretched?

⛰️

Over the weeks the darkness was my constant companion. I didn't try to fight against it, as frightening as it was. I was sick, but too afraid of my own failures to ask for help. I couldn't turn to God. He had turned his face from me long ago, so I thought. Capt. Andrews was my new god. *He* held me in his perverted grip and spoke life and death into my heart. Everything I did was to make him happy. Success or failure depended on him. Deep down I despised him as much as I despised myself, but like an addict, I continually sought praise and comfort from him, as hollow and destructive as it was.

On September 9, 2009, my 24th birthday, I stood outside the battalion TOC, listening to yet another heartless rebuke from Capt. Andrews for failing to meet his standards. Whenever he spoke all life in my body rushed out of me like a punctured basketball until I was utterly deflated. As his angry faced twitched in barely controlled rage my legs faltered underneath me and I collapsed against a metal shipping container, sliding down onto the dusty rocks. The dam holding my sanity in had been weakened from months of constant mind games and a feverish operational pace. Finally, in a violent torrent, it broke loose.

"I don't want to live anymore," I sobbed in despair to Capt. Andrews, who stood over me angrily with his hands on his hips. "I've been thinking about hurting myself for a while." Tears streamed down my face and dropped off my chin onto my M4 rifle, making dark spots on its barrel and the dusty rocks under my feet. Each time we went out on a convoy I would hope to a God that I didn't think existed anymore that he would let me get blown up. I would rather have lost a limb and spent the next several months in a hospital bed miles away than continue to live as a captive to the monster commander. I was too afraid to take my own life, but certainly didn't want to live anymore, not like that.

"Get the f*** up off the ground!" he whispered loudly, his face beginning to twitch. "You're making a scene and embarrassing me. Everyone can see you here being a f****** baby! If it's that bad then go see the chaplain. But get the f*** up right now! Just go back to your tent and pull yourself together. You're not fit to work anymore today."

I called him a series of disgusting names before hoisting myself up off the rocks. I was desperate for any sort of understanding or human empathy but wasn't going to find it here. No one was trustworthy, not even the Chaplain, who was frequently drunk and was buddies with Capt. Andrews. I pulled my hat down low over my eyes and stumbled on weak, trembling legs back to my bunk. It was mid-afternoon and most soldiers, save for one or two sleeping before their night shift, were out working. Grateful for the privacy of my poncho wall and the roar of the air conditioning unit outside the tent I laid down and wept quietly, soaking my pillow with tears. *Happy birthday to me*, I thought bitterly, before falling into an exhausted sleep.

Shortly after my breakdown, Capt. Andrews gave me a new assignment. John had to go back to the states on R&R and I would take his place in Zabul Province at FOB Wolverine. The LST needed an officer's leadership and with things the way they were, it was in his best interest to send me away for a few weeks. I was grateful for a change of scenery and to be away from the toxic environment on KAF, though I felt under equipped to command an entire 50-person LST by myself.

Just days later I climbed on to a Chinook helicopter headed for Zabul with my bags in hand. I watched the brown desert and the sprawl of Kandahar City disappear from a hole in the floor of the craft. A section of the bottom of the helicopter had been removed to reveal a large metal attachment, by which the crew could pick up a sling-rigged bundle for transport. Through the small portal I saw the neat grid of irrigated fields and an occasional herd of camels in the otherwise scarce landscape. I watched absentmindedly until it was time to land, wondering passively what the days ahead would hold.

Chapter 4

The Hen

The Chinook touched down on the gravel landing zone, and I made a hasty exit with my duffle and rucksack in tow. Ssg. Grant, the NCO in charge showed me to the female sleep tent and gave a brief tour of the base. It was much cooler than Kandahar, a welcome change, and a low chain of snow-peaked mountains provided a scenic backdrop. After dropping my bags, I made my way to the operations center to report in to Maj. Rodriguez, the infantry battalion executive officer who would be my new boss for the time being. Inside the expansive plywood building, I found his office and knocked on his open door. He was sitting at his computer and turned to face me, eyes widening in surprise.

"Sir, I'm your new LST commander until Lt. Greene gets back from R&R," I said somewhat awkwardly. Immediately, Maj. Rodriguez sprang from his chair and began yelling loudly at no one in particular.

"I can't believe they sent me a f****** female!" he sputtered. "You need to get the f*** off my FOB! I'm calling Jefferson right now so he can take you back. The last thing I need is a hen running around with my cocks." As he spoke Maj. Rodriguez snatched the phone receiver off his desk and began scrolling through the call log, trying to find Lt. Col. Jefferson's number.

"Sir, do you want logistical support or not?" I asked resignedly. "I'm all you have right now. John isn't coming back for several weeks." It was obvious that neither one of us was in on the big joke. I could picture Lt. Col. Jefferson and Maj. Andrews having a good laugh in anticipation of my arrival at Wolverine, high fiving each other over the news that Maj. Rodriguez had lost his cool at me. They had probably put money down on how long I would last there. What had seemed like a great opportunity for professional development had quickly turned into a farce.

"I'll deal with you later, lieutenant," he spat, a little too close to my face. "Now get the f*** out of my TOC and off my FOB!" He didn't have to convince me. Without looking back, I walked hurriedly back out into the warm day and towards the motor pool where the LST was working, getting their trucks ready for a mission. Ssg. Grant immediately started laughing.

"You meet the XO, LT?" he asked with a grin in his trademark West Virginia drawl. "He tell you to get the f*** off his FOB?"

"Yep, he did," I replied.

"Well pack your bag and let's go. We've got an overnight resupply mission to COP Crazyhorse this afternoon. Wanna come along?" he asked. I nodded.

"He'll cool off. He's like that to everyone."

I packed a quick overnight bag and made my way back to the motor pool where the convoy was staging. Combat Outpost Crazyhorse, or *Crazy* for short was an hour or two away, depending on traffic, via convoy, in the Shajoy District. The infantry battalion's C Company was operating out of the small, primitive base and desperately needed a food, water and ammo resupply. The convoy left shortly before sunset, charting a slow course through winding gravel roads and into the bustling city of Qalat. Locals were beginning to prepare their evening meals, and the local markets were a flurry of turbaned men and passive donkeys pulling carts.

We arrived at COP Crazy, a dusty, mud-walled compound, just after dark. The only light came from a smoldering burn pit that smelled of human waste and the occasional flash of a red lens on a soldier's headlamp. The cook on the camp offered us leftovers from a heat-and-serve MRE. In the darkness, I heard soldiers whispering.

"Is that a girl?"

"Did they bring a chick with them?"

The C Company commander, Capt. Marshall, quickly interrupted the chatter. "Knock it off, gentlemen!" Then, turning to me, he said, "Sorry, you're the first and only woman who's ever been on this COP." I smiled back weakly through the darkness, wondering what I was doing there.

That night, the LST slept in their respective trucks, with feet propped up on open doors and heads drowsily lolling over the steel radio mounts between seats as we all tried to get comfortable. Sleep was evasive. As soon as you found a comfortable position and dozed off it suddenly became unbearable. A few drivers ventured high on top of their trucks with their sleeping bags, only to scramble down a few hours later as several stray bullet rounds snapped overhead.

What was supposed to be only a two-week stint in Zabul Province turned into a month, with no projected end in sight. Maj. Rodriguez eventually came around and realized that if he sent me home he wasn't going to get any more logistical support. He still frequently yelled at me to get off his FOB, but only in a way that suggested it were his favorite catchphrase and not a threat.

My sleep improved greatly, and I slept like a baby every night, even on an issued cot. I was in my sleeping bag by 9:30 pm and awake at 6:45 on the dot without an alarm. I napped for an hour or so every afternoon, making up for lost time. The sleep helped revive my weary mind. My constant darkness lightened to gray and was almost bearable out in the cool mountain air. I knew when I returned to KAF they would come back in full force, but for the time being I did the best to unburden myself.

Capt. Andrews still managed to occasionally keep a tight rein on me from Kandahar. I suspected he had informants at FOB Wolverine who watched my every move and reported back to him. Once, he called me in the middle of the night on my Roshan phone, screaming profanities and accusing me of sleeping around. Word had gotten back to him that a Sergeant Major had leant me his fleece jacket while the LST was stranded overnight at COP Crazy. His compassionate gesture on a sub-freezing night had somehow planted a seed of perception that we were sleeping together. Capt. Andrews assailed me with accusations until I was near tears. I could practically hear his lips trembling in anger. Gratefully, the call cut out and I was off the hook until morning when we picked up the unpleasant conversation again. I felt the familiar cloud of speculation start to break me down, so I isolated myself. If I didn't talk to anyone besides my Soldiers, then no one could gossip about me.

I went on every convoy with the LST, which delivered supplies to remote corners of Zabul Province, where the infantry companies and a field artillery battery operated out of small, austere outposts. When I wasn't going on mission, I stayed in my tent or the aid station where the kind medical company commander, also a woman, had let me set up shop with my computer. She and her empathetic 1st Sgt. were small, comforting lights in an otherwise dense fog of a combat zone deployment.

One late night in October, I awoke to someone yelling outside the female sleep tent for me to wake up. I grabbed my headlamp and stumbled outside. The glow of my watch said it was after 1:00 a.m. A Specialist I recognized as Maj. Rodriguez's driver told me I was wanted in the TOC. I grabbed socks and running shoes and made the quarter mile trek in the dark to Maj. Rodriguez's office, wondering what he could possibly need at that hour. My gut knotted in anticipation. He was sitting in his office chair, wearing a short navy blue bathrobe and slippers and staring at a large laminated map on the wall. I hoped he had shorts on underneath his robe.

"LT we've got a mission for you and your guys," he says without taking his eyes off the map. "It's a refuel mission and part of a big operation the companies have going on right now." He wanted me to lead the mission and was giving me his personal armored MRAP[5] as a command vehicle. We would leave first thing in the morning along with an LST fuel truck and head to COP Crazy where we would stage for the mission

I went to wake up Ssg. Grant, who hadn't actually gone to bed yet. He and several other LST soldiers were playing video games in their tent. I gave him the mission brief, and he rounded up the team for the next morning.

Overnight puddles had frozen over, marking the first freeze of the season. The sun rose bright and clear, making the thick layer of frost on the tents sparkle. My crew and I met up in the motor pool and

---

[5] Mine Resistant Ambush Protected vehicle, a top-heavy armored military truck with explosion-deflecting properties

checked out Maj. Rodriguez's truck, making sure everything was in working order before we left for the mission. He wanted me to sign a hand receipt for the truck, essentially making it my property temporarily. If anything happened to it on the mission he would be absolved of responsibility.

The MRAP had a remote weapons system, meaning the gunner could sit inside the vehicle and operate the weapon with a joystick and thermal video screen, as opposed to sitting up in a turret, exposed. The private manning the .50 cal tested the system.

"Uh, ma'am, this weapon isn't going to fire," he shouted from the top of the truck.

"What do you mean?" I yelled back over the rumbling diesel engine.

"It's missing the entire piece that connects the weapon to the remote!"

I ran inside the TOC to find Maj. Rodriguez and let him know I wouldn't sign for his truck unless every piece was accounted for. The captain manning the TOC barred me from seeing him. Maj. Rodriguez was busy and didn't care that our broken weapon would make us sitting ducks out on the mission – we had to leave and leave *now*. I could almost hear him yelling at the captain to tell us to *get the f*** off his FOB*. I thought the inoperable weapon was a bad omen for the operation, and his willingness to send us defenseless into harm's way enraged me. At least we had a security element with us. Still, I didn't feel good about his decision. I vindictively crumpled up the unsigned hand receipt and tossed it under my seat. Whatever happened to the truck was his problem, not mine.

The convoy loitered at COP Crazy for several hours until the sun faded into black, then followed a crawling convoy of engineers in route clearance vehicles across the dark countryside to the location where the major operation was taking place. The three infantry companies were rooting out Taliban insurgents on the backside of a sharp ridge of mountains. As LST Soldiers tactically refueled the infantry vehicles in near darkness, we watched as bright white illumination rounds fired on the other side of the ridgeline hovered eerily overhead, silhouetting the jagged peaks in front of us. After a few hours, the refuel portion of the mission was complete, and my crew rallied with the fuel truck, two Stryker vehicles from C Company and our escort vehicles to head home.

We followed the American escort vehicles from the 82nd Airborne Division along small back roads through a small, mud village. It was still and pitch black in the dead of night. The Strykers were too wide to snake between the narrow compound walls, and we were forced to turn around and go back the way we came. While we were turning around, our escorts suddenly vanished, sending a weak excuse over the radio that they had other places to be. Their blue icons on my tracking screen slowly jumped away until they were out of the grid. The convoy was down to four vehicles, and only two had functioning weapon systems. Eventually we got turned around, only after getting miserably stuck in deep sand, which took nearly an hour to free the MRAP from.

At last we were on our way, saving time and miles by cutting across what appeared to be open country, heading towards COP Crazy. The small village roads were too dangerous this time of night without route clearance vehicles to detect IEDs. The convoy drove in blackout mode with all their headlights off, relying on night vision devices to navigate. After only a few minutes we realized our folly – what looked like open country was actually a grid of crop fields, criss-crossed by deep irrigation ditches. Suddenly, the MRAP went airborne with a terrifying jolt. We had hit a deep ditch at 35 miles an hour. As the truck crashed down the driver screamed and my face hit the screen in front of me, protected only by my helmet falling forward over the bridge of my nose. The truck rolled a few yards forward and came to a grinding halt on a small downhill slope.

I got out with my red lens headlamp to assess the damage. The platoon leader from C Company got out of his Stryker and met me in front of the MRAP. The front wheels were facing opposite directions, and a thick inky river of oil was spreading down the hill and soaking into the sand. Underneath, the front left axle, as thick as a tree trunk, had separated entirely from the wheel. A rod had gone straight through the oil pan, completely demolishing it. We weren't going anywhere. After nearly two hours of pleading with nearby U.S. forces and waiting for help to arrive, a wrecker truck and quick reaction force from COP Crazy finally found their way to us and recovered the damaged MRAP.

It was nearing first light when my crew and I climbed into the back of one of the Stryker vehicles, cold, hungry and grateful the worst was over. The heat in the vehicle was broken and it was freezing inside. Before I knew it my head was bobbing as sleep overtook me. Several minutes into our trip back to the COP, the vehicle commander called me up to his video screen, which looked out in front of his Stryker.

"Hey ma'am, your truck is on its side," he said pointing to the monitor. The convoy stopped and several of us got out to assess the damage. In the faint light of breaking dawn, we could see Maj. Rodriguez's MRAP rolled on its side in a ditch, still attached to the wrecker truck. The narrow goat trail we were driving on had given way under the weight of the heavy armor, sending it rolling over into a narrow wadi. *Good Lord, can anything else go wrong tonight?* I thought to myself. In the still silence of the morning the call to prayer suddenly crackled over loudspeakers in the nearby village. The chanting refrain provided a haunting backdrop as the crew of mechanics hurried to right the MRAP so we could be on our way. By the time the orange sun broke the horizon we were bumping over dirt roads, holding our breath that the truck would stay upright until we returned to safety.

⛰

Days later I got a call from Capt. Andrews that John was back from leave and would be on his way back to FOB Wolverine shortly. It was time for me to return to KAF. The eight months remaining in the deployment may as well have been a lifetime. I didn't know how I would survive it. I didn't want to stay at Wolverine and deal with Maj. Rodriguez and his bathrobe ambushes and constant outbursts, but I also didn't want to go back to KAF and under the soul-crushing control of Capt. Andrews. Either way, there was no winning, only *surviving*. I walked up to the TOC to let Maj. Rodriguez know I was leaving soon.

He didn't take the news well and told me I wasn't going anywhere. I was *his* officer, and he got the final say in where I went. Not wanting to stay and fight a losing battle, I told him to call Lt. Col. Jefferson and take it up with him. I had been a pawn in their game since day one, so my opinion was of little value in the decision to stay or return. In his usual fashion, Maj. Rodriguez screamed at me to *get the f**** out of his TOC. I rolled my eyes as I left, making my way down to the motor pool to talk to SSgt. Grant. The door to the TOC swung open wide, slamming against the outside wall. Maj. Rodriguez charged out, running down the hill at me. I stopped in my tracks, afraid of what hell he was about to unleash on me.

"Let's get this straight, lieutenant, you work for *me!*" he bellowed inches from my face, pounding his chest with a closed fist. "I don't give a f*** what your commander says. You go when I tell you to go, and you stay when I tell you to stay! Is that clear? Now get the f*** off my FOB!"

I felt rage rising in my chest, threatening to manifest itself as tears. I willed myself to hold back the torrent. Maj. Rodriguez turned on his heel and walked back to the direction of the TOC. Down the hill I walked, now in a bewildered funk, to talk to Staff Sgt. Grant. I told him the news and how Maj. Rodriguez lost his temper.

He chuckled and said, "Why do you think we stay down here in the motor pool all the time, LT?"

A few days later, a Chinook dropped off John at FOB Wolverine and picked me up to return to KAF. We waved goodbye to each other in quick passing on the landing zone. Capt. Andrews said to wait for a convoy from the BSB to come pick me up in a few days while they dropped off supplies, but I really didn't want to push my luck with Maj. Rodriguez any further. Defying Capt. Andrews' orders was a bold move, but I didn't want to stick around for any more excitement.

Chapter 5

Getting By

The late afternoon sun was getting low in the cool November sky when the helicopter landed at KAF. I called the A Company command post from inside the passenger terminal, hoping to get a ride across the base with my bags. Andy answered the phone, surprised that I was back already. He suspected the commander wasn't going to be happy that I was popping up unannounced. Capt. Andrews needed the constant ability to control when and where I went.

Andy came to get me, which I felt was probably a bad idea considering we were forbidden to be alone with each other. He didn't care though and continued to provoke Capt. Andrews every chance he could get. Andy was untouchable because he didn't care what anyone thought about him. He had a long career behind him already and had nothing to lose. His wife, a sweet southern woman named Genevieve, had called me before I was sent away, letting me know that she had my back and I was invited over for dinner when we all got back. They were a seasoned military couple that knew all the ins and outs of deployed life.

We pulled into the A Company area, and on cue, Capt. Andrews immediately saw us and elevated the situation to a critical level. He browbeat Andy and I for willfully being seen together, and me separately for not following his orders to wait for the BSB convoy to get me. The familiar cloud of heaviness and submission rolled in heavily. Things were just as they were when I left. I don't know why I expected them to be any different.

The pace of missions didn't slow down over the course of the winter months like we expected them to. Typically, Taliban fighters cross into Pakistan during the colder months to regroup and plan operations for the next fighting season. October had been the deadliest month in the Afghan war to date, and our brigade suffered devastating losses on the battlefield that summer and fall. The BSB was responsible for extricating all the destroyed vehicles from the battlefield and returning them to KAF for repair or retrograde. Most of the armored vehicles that came back were just burned out hulls, having caught fire in massive IED attacks. They sat in the motor pool, barely hidden behind makeshift walls, a dark reminder of the cost of combat. The infantry battalions especially were reeling from casualty after casualty.

A Company continued to roll out of the gate of KAF, bound for the far corners of southern Afghanistan delivering supplies. As long as soldiers needed supplies, we continued to deliver them. More and more frequently, I was assigned to lead the convoys. I finally received my first promotion, pinning on 1st Lieutenant at the end of November. It felt good to not stand out as a rookie gold bar anymore.

I loved my truck crew dearly, and they kept me sane on our missions. My driver, Specialist Solara, was a young soldier from Guam, quiet and gritty behind the wheel of the MRAP, expertly navigating the perilous terrain of blown out stretches of roads, potholed goat trails, and the occasional river crossing with dark humor and steady nerves. Private First-Class Carpenter, a native of Hawaii, rounded out our team as my gunner. Carpenter was an underrated soldier, unable to get promoted because he could never pass the Army's weight and body fat standards. His conduct and intellect were irreproachable and his light, childlike sense of humor buoyed the mood on even the most tense convoy missions.

Solara and Carpenter would tell stories over their headset mics as we bumped down desert trails into the far reaches of Afghanistan, recounting ghost encounters and superstitions from their respective islands. We howled with laughter over jokes and absurd stories, loopy with sleep deprivation on our late night returns back to KAF.

Carpenter found a way to rig a rice cooker to the truck's power system, and we had fresh sticky rice, spam and canned oysters with hot sauce as a reward when we reached our destinations. We were an unlikely trio, bonded together over hours and miles in a cramped truck on mission after mission.

But, despite the misery of daily life, there were bright spots here and there. Small doses of beauty gave me the strength to get by. There was still good left in the world. Our convoys often traveled through the bustling heart of Kandahar City during the daytime, transporting us back to another era. Women, dressed head to toe in bright blue burqas navigated the colorful market shops accompanied by men in loose trousers and tunics, topped with turbans. Bright pomegranates, apricots and bananas sat piled high on rickety carts pushed by toothless old men. Smoke from clay ovens used to make naan bread trailed fragrantly into the sky as sweat and ash-soaked bakers poked at flat loaves with long sticks. Raw cuts of meat hung in the sun on wooden poles, buzzing with flies. Livestock and carts pulled by donkeys crowded the narrow, dusty streets. Ornately decorated jingle trucks[6] carried impossibly high stacks of bicycles or lumber through the city, with passengers precariously perched on top.

We often made the return trip to KAF after sunset. The streets of the city would be peaceful and still as residents closed up shops and prepared their evening meals. As we silently navigated the empty streets, I would gaze out the tiny window of the MRAP through thick bulletproof glass in captivated wonder. Bare bulbs hung from open-sided shop ceilings illuminated the serene dioramas of darkened Kandahar. Groups of turbaned men squatted around open fires or lounged on thin burgundy cushions, breaking off pieces of naan and drinking cups of chai from small clear mugs. They scarcely paid notice to our great rumbling convoys. My mind would come alive watching the small scenes of daily life in Afghanistan.

Winter brought with it heavy rains and flooding. One particularly stormy February night, we awoke to inches of standing water in our sleep tents. KAF had severely flooded, and it was no longer safe or sanitary to stay in our overcrowded tents. We moved into

---

[6] Dozens of hanging metal flourishes on the bright cargo trucks make a jingling noise as it passes

a large building with two massive open bays – one for the men and one for the women. There were flushing toilets and private showers and it felt like absolute luxury.

I no longer battled against the cloud of darkness around me like I had before. I was numb and resigned to its oppression. Capt. Andrews still had his claws deeply into me, puppeting me around as he saw fit, subjecting me to his soul-crushing manipulation to *make me a better leader*. I could hardly go to the bathroom without his express permission. During missions he would message me on our navigation system constantly when I was convoy commander, critiquing my every move and radio call. When we arrived at our destination he would have a list of things that I did wrong. Despite the fact that I was the go-to lieutenant for the most challenging convoy missions in the battalion, Capt. Andrews never cut me a break.

Andy was moved to another base, given a hastily made-up position as an excuse to make the gossip about us go away. Sgt. Michaels returned home after an investigation revealed she had forged documents allowing herself and several others to receive promotions. Even though the drama had died down, I was still miserable. The mission tempo was relentless, and I spent nearly 18 hours a day in the command post as the ringleader of the circus that was A Company.

I was able to get through each day by stuffing my hurt as deeply down into my chest as I could. The intensity of my suffering scared me, but I was too ashamed to let my family or friends back home know I was struggling so deeply. I didn't think they could bear the burden of hearing about my abuse and assumed they, too, would heap blame on me. Still, despite my best efforts to turn off my emotions, part of my heart remained tender and raw.

⛰

In March, nine months after arriving in Afghanistan, I finally got the opportunity to take 15 days of R&R at home. I contemplated a quiet vacation by myself but decided to go home to Illinois to see my family. They worried about me endlessly and needed to see first-hand that I was okay. My family and friends met me at the airport with cheers, handmade signs and teary-eyed hugs of relief. I had never been so glad to see my parents in my entire life. We left the airport and made it just in time to surprise my youngest sister, Madeline, at her middle school volleyball game. I was still in my uniform, disheveled from the hours of international travel.

The two weeks went by quickly, with most of my family members, including my three sisters and young niece, making an appearance for several days. We engaged in our usual sisterly shenanigans, causing loud ruckuses at the dinner table and generally disturbing the peace of our parents' quiet suburban home. I felt refreshed by the time with family, but still not entirely myself. Returning back to civilization in the middle of war was tough. I felt like I was hiding behind a façade of who I thought I should be and couldn't quite separate my mind from the combat zone.

At the end of the two weeks I said goodbye to my parents at the small local airport. They were teary and anxious, but I was ready to get back to work and finish out the last three months of deployment. Dry-eyed, I left them in the lobby and boarded a plane back into hell.

⛰

A Company stayed busy right up until the day we packed up to leave Afghanistan. We took on several challenging missions, including the task of escorting hundreds of Afghan National Army forces into Helmand Province for the historic Battle of Marjah[7]. In April, less than three months before returning home, the BSB accepted the challenge of conducting a ground resupply[8] to U.S. Special Forces troops on a small firebase in the lethal Sangin district of Helmand Province next to the Helmand River, known for its opium fields and deadly fighting grounds. No coalition forces had ever attempted a ground resupply in the Helmand River Valley before – it was heavily laden with IEDs and nests of Taliban fighters, and had already claimed dozens of American and British lives.

---

[7] Also known as Operation Moshtarak, at the time was the largest joint offensive campaign in Afghanistan to date since the fall of the Taliban. Two Soldiers from the BSB earned Purple Heart Medals after an IED attack during the operation.

[8] To date, the BSB's convoy is the largest ground resupply ever conducted in the OEF war

The village of Sangin, just outside the firebase, desperately needed a new bridge to cross the Helmand River by foot and vehicle. Their stone bridge had been blasted by an IED placed in a boat and floated downstream. All that remained of it was a crumbling footpath over the river, which split the small village in half, making travel and commerce difficult. A U.S. Army Engineer company would provide the bridge-building assets, and we would provide the escort through the desert. A British unit joined in on the operation, hoping to resupply its nearby troops once the convoy made it through the valley.

The convoy, led by an American route clearance team, departed at sunrise and headed northward across the open desert toward Sangin, kicking up great clouds of dust as it went. The U.S. firebase was less than 10 miles away, so the trip should have been a relatively short one by all accounts. But, when we had only moved a few hundred meters by the time the sun had risen high overhead, I suspected something wasn't right.

By mid-afternoon, the convoy had only moved marginally further toward our destination. The route clearance team encountered a field of IEDs blocking our route north and was required to clear them before we could continue. It was a delicate job that demanded patience and precision. Before long a call came on the radio – one of the lead British vehicles had been hit by an IED. The passengers were uninjured, but the vehicle wasn't able to continue on. The vehicle recovery process took another chunk of precious time. Soon after we had inched forward a couple hundred feet another call came up on the radio. The Brits hit another IED, which decimated the vehicle and injured at least two of their soldiers. They needed immediate medical evacuation. We waited tensely in place while a MEDEVAC helicopter arrived on scene, carrying away the wounded soldiers for treatment.

Within one hour the convoy triggered two more explosions, bringing the blast count to four. Meanwhile, the route clearance team had already cleared five additional IEDs in their place and found several others, marking them with red glow sticks. The entire route was littered with buried explosives. It was no wonder why no coalition force had attempted a ground resupply. It was suicidal. Scanners covertly monitoring Taliban radio channels intercepted chatter between two insurgents watching our progress through the valley from the nearby mountains. They referred to our vehicles as "tanks" and wondered what kind of weapon they could use to eliminate us. We were sitting ducks in the open desert with high ground on both sides. Insurgents could have easily attacked the entire convoy with no way for us to escape. If we moved, the IEDs would get us. If we stayed put, we were fish in a barrel. I looked out my window at the sun beginning to set behind the shimmering mountains. Their golden beauty now seemed sinister and threatening. We had practiced our battle drills time and again before every single mission, but in the face of an imminent threat they seemed useless. We couldn't go anywhere.

Suddenly American Blackhawk helicopters roared overhead on their way east from another mission nearby. Capt. Andrews immediately called them on their frequency, requesting their help to visually check our route up to Sangin. Our mission had been refused any sort of air support, and now we were desperate. The pilot answered back that he was very low on fuel but agreed to do what he could to help out until forced to return to KAF and refuel. The Blackhawk turned north and made two low passes over the route through the Helmand River Valley. There were no visible threats that he could see. At least we knew we weren't driving into an ambush.

Night fell quickly as the long convoy inched through the deep moon dust. We had hardly covered any significant ground and were already more than 12 hours into the mission. The route clearance team was still working feverishly to clear a safe berth through the desert, continuing to mark each IED with a red glow stick. The team also marked our path forward between the IEDs with white glow sticks, which frequently became obscured by the thick clouds of dust the trucks kicked up when we moved along in short spurts. The stop-and-go continued through the night. I fought to stay awake when we stopped in place for minutes or even hours at a time.

Nearing the 3 o'clock hour, the route clearance team called on the radio. They had encountered a particularly large field of explosives, and the path through it was narrow, winding down and around a steep hill. The team leader advised extreme caution. Our convoy was already experiencing a shrouded path from the thick clouds of dust, making driving conditions harrowing. My driver took the steep turn down the hill too quickly and I suddenly wished my usual driver, Solara, had been able to come with us on the mission. Her driving was rock steady. I gripped the handle in the truck above my head as Carpenter barked words of caution from the gunner's turret. MRAPs were notoriously top-heavy and prone to rollover accidents, and we were leaning pretty far to the right. After a tense moment we cleared the steep hill. The dust momentarily cleared to reveal an expanse of red glow sticks on either side of the truck – dozens of them. My breath caught in my throat as we crawled by, struggling to keep the safe white glow sticks in sight in the cloud of dust.

That was the longest ten mile trip of my life – 37 hours after setting out across the desert, we finally made it to Sangin. The adrenaline that carried us through the last two days quickly wore off after our safe arrival, leaving us famished and desperate for sleep. The plan was to refuel the convoy trucks and rest overnight, allowing the American engineer company enough time to build their bridge over the Helmand River. We would return soon afterwards, retracing our steps across the desert, before insurgents had time to plant more IEDs along the route.

Our plans quickly changed when we realized the U.S. route clearance team left along with the British convoy as soon as we arrived safely. Without the route clearance team, we couldn't go anywhere. The BSB had no IED clearing capabilities, and we could be in bad shape if we attempted to travel back across the desert alone. We could only wait. The BSB headquarters on KAF would come up with a new plan to get us out. Until then, we had all the time in the world.

The American engineer company took two days to build a beautiful Bailey bridge across the milky green Helmand River, reconnecting the severed halves of the village. I watched in amazement through the lens of my camera as they toiled under the hot sun in full protective gear, with weapons slung across their backs, building the impressive bridge. It was the first bridge of its kind built in combat since the Vietnam War and was wide and sturdy enough for vehicle use. As soon as the construction was completed, a small girl with a saffron colored scarf across her shoulder and her infant brother in her arms crossed the bridge, looking fearfully towards the soldiers in uniform who lingered nearby. Next, a young boy expertly led his large herd of goats across, swinging a long stick as he went. Tentatively, a family in a car approached the bridge and crossed carefully to the other side. Soon, merchants with carts and young children with water jugs in hand hustled back and forth across the new bridge, marveling at the new expanse.

We stayed in Sangin for 11 days, sleeping on cots next to our trucks under the open sky and washing our clothes in buckets. Soldiers strung up parachutes over top of the trucks to provide a bit of shade from the intense heat. We passed the time challenging a scraggly bunch of barefoot Afghan National Army soldiers to a volleyball match, only to get annihilated by their surprising skills.

Special operations soldiers from the UAE occupied a small compound on the firebase, and they invited the officers over several times for food and drink. Their luxuriously air-conditioned tents were outfitted with rich red carpets, cushioned benches and satellite TV which broadcasted European football matches. A glass drink cooler in the corner was filled with fizzy fruit-flavored drinks in glass bottles, which we gratefully guzzled after days of sipping on dusty bottles of warm water from the back of our trucks. They set out plates filled with bunches of crisp green grapes, berries and exotic fruits I'd never even heard of. The Emirates had an unlimited budget, even out in the remote desert, and received helicopter resupplies regularly. We were grateful for their hospitality and a break from the heat.

Finally, on the 11th day, a new route clearance team made their way across the desert, reaching us in a matter of a few hours. They had found a new route through the valley with significantly fewer IEDs. The route was most likely used as a Taliban trade route to navigate the fertile river valley and resupply their insurgents. The convoy returned to KAF in an equally short time, grateful for the unhindered route and safe passage.

A couple weeks later I ate dinner with several fellow officers who had been part of the same ROTC program as me in college. We laughed at the wild chance that five of us were assigned to the same base at the same time. Two of them, Josh and Josiah, were Blackhawk pilots and had been my first team leaders as a freshmen cadet. For an entire year they mentored me weekly, teaching me how to march and wear my uniform correctly. Now we were in a combat zone together, doing things we never could have dreamed of as college students in small Illinois towns. I told them about our crazy mission to Sangin, and how a Blackhawk pilot, flying on his last fuel reserves, had helped clear the route for us in the middle of a hellish day.

"Was the convoy commander's call sign Alpha 6?" Josiah asked. I nodded.

"That was me! I was the guy in the Blackhawk." My mouth gaped before I could speak. My friend, who I didn't even know was deployed until a couple hours prior, had been our guardian angel that day. The significance of the event brought me close to tears. *Someone* was looking out for us.

The reality of going home started to feel real when our replacements began to arrive at KAF and gradually integrated into our day-to-day operations and missions. I marveled somewhat sardonically at how well-rested and cheerful our replacements seemed. *They'll get beaten down soon enough*, I thought. I snapped at one of the new platoon leaders from the unit replacing us when he asked if he really needed to wear body armor on convoy missions. He thought it was uncomfortable and not entirely necessary. Apparently, he had no idea how many soldiers our brigade had lost to IEDs. He looked at me sheepishly after I set him straight. Twelve months in country had given me a hard edge, but I really didn't care who I offended at that point.

More than willingly I handed my XO responsibilities over to my replacement, breathing a sigh of relief to be done leading convoys and generally managing the chaos of A Company. I even caught up on season one of *Glee*, which I watched captivated from my laptop on my bed. I was proud of everything I endured and accomplished, and that at the end of it all, I was still standing.

Chapter 6

Home

It was after midnight on June 28, 2010 when the plane landed at McChord Airfield, Washington, 366 days after leaving it. The cool summer air was deliciously fragrant as we stepped out onto the tarmac to see a long stream of uniformed soldiers waiting to shake our hands and welcome us home. Finally. *Finally.* I was back in my beloved state, in one piece. It took a few hours for all of us to turn in our weapons and complete all the necessary processing. Finally, near 2 a.m. they paraded us into a gym on post, placing us behind a moveable divider on the basketball court. On the other side, mobs of friends and family and cranky children up past their bedtime waited to see their loved ones returning from war. My college friend and fellow Army officer, Aaron, was going to meet me there. He had been deployed when I arrived at Fort Lewis the year prior and his wife Katie, my college roommate, had taken care of me. Now Katie was deployed, finishing out a yearlong stint in Kuwait. He and Katie were my only friends in the state. I was just happy to have someone there to meet me.

Aaron picked me up in a bear hug when the curtain lifted and loaded my duffle bags into his car. I didn't have a place to stay, so he had offered up his home for me. It was long after 3 a.m. when we finally got to his house. He made me a turkey sandwich, introducing me to avocado for the first time. I chewed gratefully under the kitchen lights, enjoying the quiet and the feel of carpet under my bare feet. Aaron graciously slept on the couch so I could enjoy a real bed for the night.

I was wide awake by 7:00 a.m. scrolling through my phone looking at nearby apartments available for rent. Although I love Katie and Aaron dearly, I hated to impose on their hospitality very long. They were the sort of people that won't rest until your every need was met, and I knew Aaron would go above and beyond to accommodate me, which I didn't feel I deserved or required. More than anything, I wanted my own space to process and decompress. With all that had happened I felt like I could sit in a quiet room alone for weeks on end and never grow tired of it. I wanted something to feel like home.

⛰

Shortly after returning my parents and younger sisters, Madeline and Laura, came out to Washington to visit for several days. Their presence was soothing and welcome. We hiked together in the Olympic National Forest and played with my recently adopted kitten, Finn. We had lots of fun, but I was emotionally fractured underneath, unsure of how to fix myself. I wanted to be back home in my bed and to sleep for days on end. As much as I enjoyed their company I was glad when they left to return to Illinois. I vaguely suspected they knew I wasn't myself, and I didn't want them to see too far into my brokenness. After they left, I took another three weeks of leave in hopes it would be what I needed to recover.

Towards the end of my leave, Laura and I took a five-day trip to Puerto Rico in hopes that a warm, relaxing vacation would be what my nerves needed. Laura was about to start her senior year of college and was endlessly game for an adventure. We had a wonderful time climbing waterfalls and exploring the rainforest around San Juan, but all I wanted to do was lay in bed. It took concerted effort to go out each day, even though white sand and endless blue ocean beckoned. At the end of our time together I found myself grateful for the isolation of a long flight back to Seattle and an empty apartment.

⛰

After returning from leave I took on a new job on the BSB staff, working in the plans and operations section. My new boss was mild, but slightly irritating, although benign at his core. I constantly bucked his authority, unwilling to let him think he had any power over me. Capt. Andrews stayed in A Company for a while, but eventually changed jobs, staying on post. He continued to show up for battalion ceremonies and events, reminding me that I was not really free from his grasp. I worked hard at my new job on staff, which provided very few challenges other than staying busy. Even the brigade's post-deployment reset time moved at a frantic pace. After leave, we went right back into an all-consuming training cycle, getting ready for another Afghanistan deployment less than 18 months later. The American military machine never stopped moving, and we were in the chute.

I began attending a church in town, at the beckoning of Aaron. He played guitar on the worship team some Sundays and pestered me to join the team. They desperately needed a keyboard player to join their band, so Aaron had talked up my piano playing talents to the team, much to my chagrin. We had played together in college a couple times, and I was decidedly mediocre at best. I was irritated by his undeserved belief in my skills and did *not* want to play in a worship band. Inside, I didn't even want to go to church but felt the need to keep up my Christian façade. Maybe if I looked outwardly churchy, then people wouldn't ask me if I was doing okay. I could put on a good face for a few months and pretend like I was in a good place with God.

Each time I took the stage under the bright spotlights, I felt like a total phony. *If these people only knew what kind of person I was they wouldn't want me up here.* I was no shining example of a Christian. I didn't even know if I still believed in God, but there I was, leading worship on Sunday mornings like a complete hypocrite, saying and doing all the right things. Behind my mask I was deeply wounded and frightened of who I had become.

The people on the worship team and in the congregation continually complemented me on my playing, telling me I was *anointed*, and that God was playing through me. That caused me more pain than if they'd told me I was terrible and booted me off the team. I barely practiced each week and definitely didn't feel God inspiring my music. Their praise felt wholly undeserved.

Anytime I felt a twinge of conviction in my daily life I quickly extinguished it with excuses. *That wasn't God. If He exists He doesn't want anything from me anymore.* Yet, denying God felt like a bigger leap of faith than believing in Him. However, in my state of shame and brokenness I continued to shut Him out for months on end.

On the afternoon of New Year's Eve, I sat on my couch alone, feeling the full weight of the past two years heavy on my shoulders as I looked with trepidation to the New Year. What would 2011 bring? More of the horrors of 2009 and 2010? Another deployment? Could I even continue to live this way?

I had existed for so long in the strange, dark limbo of a diminished life apart from God. I hid from Him, unwilling to let Him into the terrifying recesses of my heart – places I was too afraid to look at. I didn't trust myself and I didn't trust God. After all, hadn't He turned His back on me? Where had He been in the midst of my immense suffering, physical and emotional attacks and confusion? There couldn't be any grace left for me, a pathetic, shell of a woman who wasn't strong enough to stand up for herself.

I didn't recognize myself when I looked in the mirror. Only two years ago I had been a bright-eyed, eager lieutenant, ready to change the world. Now, the hollowness behind my eyes scared me. Whoever I was, whatever I had been, felt lost and irretrievable. The happy girl with vision and joy was long gone. I didn't know who this new Meredith was; the one who met my eyes in the mirror. I wondered who else saw through my shallow attempts to feign wholeness. I was nothing more than a fraud.

There was nothing left in me to fight. I didn't want to keep living the way I was living, but I felt completely powerless to move forward. But I feared that if something in my life didn't change soon that I would forsake God forever and fall deeper into fear and depression. Out of sheer desperation, I searched my apartment for the book my grandmother gave me – *My Utmost for His Highest*, which I had long stashed away in a bookshelf along with my Bible, hoping to hide from their conviction. But now I was in urgent need, hopeless. Tentatively, I opened it to December 31, the last page in the book, and began to read Oswald Chambers' words.

"The Lord will go before you, and the God of Israel will be your rear guard" (Isaiah 52:12). Anxiety is apt to arise when we remember our yesterdays. Our yesterdays hold broken and irreversible things for us. It is true that we have lost opportunities that will never

return, but God can transform this destructive anxiety into a constructive thoughtfulness for the future. Let the past rest, but let it rest in the sweet embrace of Christ. Leave the broken, irreversible past in His hands, and step out into the invincible future with Him.

A rush of conviction swept through me like sweet, fresh air, pushing the stagnant, putrid smog out of my soul. The past was unchangeable and rife with failure, *should haves* and deep, grieving regret. I had been living as if my future, one of ugly brokenness, had already been written for me. The enemy had perverted my vision and held me captive with lies of shame and unworthiness. *You don't deserve happiness and wholeness. It's your fault – everything. This is as good as things are going to get from here on out. You're damaged and unworthy. Look how far you've fallen! God can't use you. And you call yourself a Christian, you hypocrite.*

The light of truth exposed the hollow lies for what they were; they were desperate attempts by the enemy to keep me from walking out God's calling on my precious life. God held my future and could redeem everything that had turned to a heap of ash. I didn't have to wander in darkness anymore. Truly, I didn't have the power and strength to change, but God did, and He called me to Himself in the quietness of my apartment that afternoon. From the depths of my soul, cries flowed out to Him in desperation. I prayed the most simple and sincere prayer of my life, prostrate in front of my couch. *Lord, please help me. I don't want to live like this anymore.*

In an instant, the violent tempest in my soul settled, and all was peaceful and smooth, like glass. God spoke to the wind and waves and commanded them to *be still*. The angry black clouds evaporated and the sky became serenely gray, like the early morning just before breaking dawn. The sun was going to rise again – I could feel it coming. Hope. Then, He spoke, gently and sweetly.

I love you. I am for you. I've always been for you.

Resolutely, I envisioned myself taking His hand – I would cling to Him, deciding I was done with darkness. Never again would it take me under and drown me in shame. God loved me and was fighting for me. There was no limit to His grace and mercy. *Nothing* could separate me from His love. *Nothing.*

Immediately I called Capt. Andrews and boldly told him that

what he had done to me was wrong, and that he would never touch me again or speak to me. There was no place in my life for his abuse and manipulation. He had stolen nearly two years of my innocence and sanity. He refused to apologize, trying to convince me everything he had done was for *my* benefit, and I had been complicit in his abuse. He threatened to contact my parents through Facebook and tell them I was a whore who had slept with a married man. In that moment I felt an impermeable wall of protection drop around me, knowing God would quell any of his attempts to blackmail me. Nothing Capt. Andrews said could hurt me anymore – he had no power in my life. His threats were the final tolling bell of a darker enemy desperate to keep me from living in light and freedom. Dry eyed, I hung up the phone claimed my victory. I was truly free.

In that moment I knew God had been there all along, side by side with me in the blackest pit of hell with an outstretched hand, waiting for me to call His name. It was clear now – His great love did not condemn me. Together, we stepped into the invincible future. He would be my rear guard and He would go before me, making a way for my life.

Chapter 7

The Invincible Future

I walked into the packed church auditorium for their New Year's Eve service and for the first time since I could remember, felt unafraid. God instantly erased the murky blackness in my heart and gave me new hope, without condemnation. In that moment I really understood what David was talking about when he wrote in Psalms that God lifted him out of the mud and mire and gave him a firm place to stand. God saw into the most closed off, shame filled recesses of my heart and loved me no less. If God could love me, then so could other people. And I could love myself. I didn't fear the gazes of my friends and strangers anymore. I wasn't afraid of them really seeing me. I no longer felt like a fraud, pretending to have my life in perfect order while screaming out in broken desperation on the inside.

It was as if a brilliant light had poured into my terrifying darkness through a wide open door. For the first time I realized that small, persistent voice in my head during my darkest hours in Afghanistan was not the voice of condemnation, but the sweet voice of a God who still loved me and still had a plan and purpose for my life. The enemy had distorted it, turning it into accusations of unworthiness and failure. The overwhelming realization of God's beautiful and unearned grace flooded through me and I totally surrendered to it. I left the past behind at that moment and ran headlong into the future. I've never been one to take a lot of stock in the symbolism of a new year, but that night, December 31, 2010, I wholly embraced the opportunity to start over.

The atmosphere in the church that night quivered with electricity and a heavy sense of calming peace at the same time. Even in the packed room, I felt like I was alone there with God. The musicians and singers on stage began to play the song *Moving Forward* by

Ricardo Sanchez and I erupted unashamedly into tears, pierced by the apt words.

I'm not going back, I'm moving ahead.
I'm here to declare to you my past is over.
In you all things are made new.
I'm giving my life to Christ and I'm moving, moving forward.

The tears that flowed freely came from a place of gratitude and surrender, not the usual blackness of frustration and anger, which had been my default. I felt light and unburdened, and *alive*. I greedily ate up every morsel of grace and truth that came my way that night. My soul was so dry and desperate for God, and I felt the fresh streams of hope pour through my wasteland.

The pastor challenged each of us present to *give God a year* and fully surrender 2011 over to him. At the end of the service we received blank letters with an envelope, to write down what we were praying for this year. The church leaders would pray over the sealed letters throughout the year and mail them back to us before the next New Year. I clutched the clean white paper in my hand as I left, wondering what beauty and goodness God was going to show me the next 12 months.

All I wanted was *more*. The enemy had stolen so much peace and sanity from me I just wanted more *life*. God had given me the beautiful gift of restoration and I was ready to hit the ground running into whatever adventure awaited. My new eyes wanted to see everything there was to see and to taste the bounty of the living. I was back from the dead and hungry for life. I opened the blank letter from church and wrote down a few simple lines from a song.

We believe for even greater
We believe for more
Let Your power come upon us
We believe for more

Below it I wrote *I want more.* I sealed the letter in the envelope and scribbled my name on it, feeling excited and a little foolish, like maybe my dreams were *too* big. I was afraid of wanting too much. God had already heaped grace on me, and I was a little scared to ask for more than that. I hadn't realized yet that God was *always* for me; always working on my behalf for my good.

The peace that invaded my heart on New Year's Eve didn't leave in the days and weeks that followed. God had set me free from oppression and shame, and each day I continued to find solid ground underneath my feet. I felt as if a steel wall between the past and me had dropped solidly behind me, protecting me from the clutches of fear. At church, a young adult group called Twentysomethings met on Sunday evenings for worship and small group discussion, led by a wonderful young married couple, Tyler and Katie. Twenty-somethings became a respite for me, a place to be loved and to grow.

I began realizing I had really craved and needed safe friendships. I had hidden from spiritually healthy people for a long time, afraid that they would see right through me. At first, I thought there was no way any of these perfect people could understand the pain and struggle I had been through. If they *really* knew me or how deeply I had questioned the existence of God there was no way they could let me play the piano with Katie for worship or lead a small group discussion. My faith wasn't solid enough yet to make me a trustworthy guide, I thought.

My own perceived inferiority and unworthiness hindered the cultivation of friendships at first. I held on to a deeply rooted belief that people who actually loved God didn't fall away like I did, and maybe there was some defect inside me that would always make my relationship with God a struggle. I believed wholeheartedly in redemption, but that somehow buried deep inside grace, there was an *if* clause. *If* I didn't hold up my end of the spiritual bargain then God had every right to abandon me to ruin. A painful sliver of that lie stayed with me for a long time.

Since joining the Army, I hadn't made hardly any friends at all. There were a few people at work that I enjoyed the company of, but my heart had been so wounded that I had hidden inside myself, unable to make any meaningful human connections. But I soon found my cold heart was able to beat again and it was more than capable of empathy and connection. Katie and Tyler became steadfast friends, constantly feeding me truth without judgment. Their vulnerability with their own struggles freed me to share small parts of my own. They were imperfect humans who had deeply experienced the darkness of loss and doubt. But they were also living examples of lives redeemed.

I also met two beautiful young women through Twenty-somethings, Crystal and Mary, who both reflected quiet, fierce steadfastness and unconditional love. They unwittingly revealed my deep prejudices against Christians. Though I loved God, I assumed every other Christian around me had their lives in order and couldn't possibly experience the heartbreak of deep struggle.

Outwardly, these women made loving God seem effortless and easy, so cynically I wondered if they had ever even had a rough day in their lives. But as I got to know them, I realized in a huge way that they *did* have struggles and pain and doubts, and what God had done for them was no more or no less than what he had done for me. Like Tyler and Katie, they spoke gentle truth into my life, warming up my cold soul. Over the months God continued to unravel my bitter tapestry of judgment, weaving threads of new life into me.

⚇

Shortly after the New Year, an itchy sort of restlessness began to creep into my mind. I had been working in a staff position at the BSB since July, writing an endless string of orders and tasks for the companies. The work kept me busy but did little to engage my mind. I wanted to get out of there, to do something new and challenging. I applied for the all-Army women's basketball team, which was a *long* shot. Unsurprisingly, I didn't hear back from them. I suspected they didn't want a 5'8" forward with zero college basketball experience other than an intramural league in which I had headlined the statistics in fouls per game.

One day in March my coworker, Master Sergeant Cooper, sent me an email about an interesting opportunity. She had been one of the A Company Platoon Sergeants when we were deployed and had occasionally left me kind notes and cards on my bunk to let me know at least one person in the unit cared about me. *Ma'am, this sounds right up your alley. I think you would be perfect for this,* she wrote. I opened the PDF attachment in the email and read the title. *FEMALE SOLDIERS. BECOME A PART OF HISTORY.*

Underneath, it laid out the requirements for rank and physical fitness to be a part of the Cultural Support Team program. I easily met the standards. *Assist Special Forces and Ranger units in Afghanistan. You will be trained to think critically, interact with local Afghan women and children, and integrate as a member of an elite unit.* The next selection cycle was in May at Fort Bragg, North Carolina. I immediately hit the print button and carried the flyer into my boss' office, the paper still warm from the printer.

"I'm doing this," I said, slapping the flyer on his desk. He looked up at me, momentarily stunned, before reading it over.

"Okay, go for it. You have my blessing," he replied nonchalantly, making the sign of the cross at me. I snatched the flyer back and returned to my desk. One way or another, I was getting out of the BSB and doing something that *mattered.*

Over the next weeks I upped my physical fitness routine, carrying heavy rucksacks over several miles in the dark of the morning and lifting weights. Not getting selected was *not* an option. The CST program sounded ideal. It was everything I had wanted to do in the Army – work with elite units and be a part of what was happening on the ground in Afghanistan, not hiding behind two inches of bulletproof glass in a death trap, waiting to get blown up. And I had long felt my talents in the Army were underutilized. I wanted an actual challenge that involved more than just surviving epic proportions of adversity and making stellar excel spreadsheets.

As a woman I would never be an infantry soldier, but this was as close as I could get. After meeting the initial requirements at my unit and getting the approval of the battalion commander, I submitted my application packet to the screening board. Within days I heard back – I was on the selection roster for May.

I trained furiously for the next two months. I would *not* be the weak link at selection. I had to get selected, there was no question about it. I wanted it so badly that it never occurred to me that I might fail.

Chapter 8

Courage

My friend, Sam, picked me up outside my apartment at 3:00 a.m. for my 6:00 flight to Fayetteville, North Carolina on a cool morning in early May. I dropped my heavy bags in her trunk and clutched a manila folder filled with my travel orders and important documents in my hand as I got into the front seat. I had packed and unpacked and repacked my rucksack and duffle bag time and time again, checking it against the selection packing list I received weeks earlier. If the selection cadre wanted to kick me out, it wouldn't be because I had forgotten something on the packing list.

I had invested in a new pair of custom designed Nike Frees after reading on the packing list we weren't allowed to bring black athletic shoes with us. My only running shoes were black. I spent almost an hour trying out different color combinations on the Nike website, finally settling on a gold and turquoise pair. I could even add a custom word to the backs of the shoes. I thought about adding my name, but that seemed cheesy. What *one* word was going to be my key phrase? *Run. Run Fast? Victory. Endurance. Courage.* Yes, that was it, *courage*. In my preparation for selection I had read God's promise to Joshua, and it stuck with me. *Be strong and courageous, do not be terrified, do not be discouraged, for the Lord your God is with you wherever you go[9]*. I picked out a purple color for the thread and typed *COURAGE* into the customization bar. Courage would be my word.

I checked in to the Landmark Inn on Fort Bragg and dropped my bags in my room, which I would be sharing with another CST candidate for two nights before we headed out to Camp Mackall, an

---

[9] Joshua 1:9

Army Special Operations training area, for selection. Over 50 other women were reporting that day for selection. Most of them were in civilian clothes, and I suddenly felt self-conscious in my uniform. I was so afraid of bringing anything extra that wasn't on the packing list that I hadn't brought any regular clothes with me.

"Hey, has anyone ever told you that you look like Melanie Laurent?" a young woman in workout gear asked me as I grabbed a banana from the hotel snack bar. "You know, the girl from Inglorious Basterds?"

"Uh, no, I'm not sure who that is," I smiled, making a mental note to Google Melanie Laurent later.

That evening my temporary roommate arrived, a diminutive Army Lieutenant named Leah. She was a Military Police officer, recently returned from a deployment to Iraq where she had led patrols with her platoon of mostly male soldiers. She was warm and friendly, if not a little shy, but we bonded quickly over our mutual faith. Leah was just as nervous as I was, totally in the dark about what to expect over the next week, and more than a little paranoid that we were being watched and evaluated before selection even began. A steady stream of Green Berets had been coming in and out of the hotel, and we suspected they were watching us, and not only because we were a group of 50-some exceptionally fit women.

The Army cargo trucks pulled up to the hotel at 4:00 a.m. two mornings later to pick us up and take us to Camp Mackall. After a brief accountability formation, we all loaded up into the back of the tarp-covered truck beds and found a seat on the cold, metal benches lining the sides. The drivers closed the back gate and strapped down the back flap so we couldn't see out the back. The sun wasn't up yet, and it was dark in the back of the truck. We drove for what seemed like an hour, our heads bobbing in and out of sleep. Finally, we arrived at Camp Mackall, and someone opened the back truck flap, sending the early morning light streaming into our faces. A team of cadre greeted us, barking orders at us to get down out of the trucks and fall into formation.

My stomach grumbled as I fell into formation alongside the 55 other women and I suddenly wished I had eaten more than just a granola bar that morning. We were already dressed in our physical training uniforms and suspected the Army Physical Fitness Test would be our first challenge. Instead, cadre ordered us to dump out our bags on the ground. It was inventory time. They confiscated any item that wasn't on the packing list and took our cell phones and watches away. I was so paranoid about the packing list that I had left my phone at home in my apartment.

After the inventory a gruff Major led us over to a concrete pad where we were given instructions for the APFT, then ordered into complete silence. Several graders with metal counters in their hands were waiting for us. We each completed our two minutes of pushups and sit-ups while the rest of the group stood silently in line, our backs facing the women taking the test. It was silent, save for the grunting and heavy breathing of the women doing pushups and sit-ups, and the occasional hushed counting from the graders as they clicked off each repetition.

Then, we moved to a dilapidated airstrip nearby for the two-mile run. The day was already starting to get warm and the orange traffic cone at the one-mile turnaround point wavered in the haze. We took off in a jostling pack, the gazelles quickly pulling away from the group in a flash of lean, tan legs. They were obviously naturals. I usually ran toward the front of the pack on the APFT two-miler back at my unit, but these ladies weren't your average Army soldiers. They were *fast*. I finished in a respectable time of 15:15, nearly four minutes after the pack leader.

We changed into our sterilized uniforms, which we had stripped of our rank, name and unit patches. In their place was white cloth sewn onto our cargo pockets and upper sleeves designating our assigned candidate number. Our sole identification that week would be our number, written in black permanent marker. While we were there we would have no rank, no name, no status. I received number 26. Then the cadre handed out yellow timing chips to clip onto our boots. They would track us during various challenges via professional timing mats typically used at races.

Afterwards they separated us into groups of 8-10. We would do every event that week with our new squads – eating, sleeping and physical challenges. The cadre emphasized that even though we were placed into teams, the selection was an individual event. We wouldn't be graded on how we performed as a team, but only our own capabilities. I joined the group of 3rd Squad women as we dumped our gear onto cots in a large, nearby tent.

For the remainder of the week our instructions would come from a whiteboard across the rocky courtyard between two long lines of tents. A plastic analog clock hung on a nail over the board served as our only reference for the time. The rules were simple. Take all commands from the whiteboard, run everywhere you go, no stashing away food, and no sleeping unless you're told to do so. *1600hrs formation, ACUs. 35-pound ruck (dry), full Camelbak, full 2-quart and 1-quart canteens.* We hustled back to the tent and began preparing our rucksacks, running back and forth between the tent and the hanging scale across the courtyard. A dry rucksack meant water didn't count toward the overall weight of the pack. We would pack an additional five to six liters of water, which added nearly 12 pounds to the load. Additionally, we would carry "ducks," or rubber M-16 rifle replicas.

We formed up in the gravel outside the tents with our rucksacks. The afternoon sun still shone hot in the sky, and the air was muggy. An NCO with a clipboard stood on an elevated wooden platform in front of the formation.

"You will now conduct an unknown time and distance road march," he yelled into a megaphone. "You will follow the orange cones marking the route. You may not assist any other candidate or talk during the march. If you do not see an orange cone, do not make a turn on the route." He led us back out to the airstrip, which radiated the afternoon sun back into our faces and distorted the horizon.

We took off at his command. Some women took off sprinting to get ahead of the pack and some walked, conserving energy for however long the march would take. I decided on a moderate shuffle to get out of the mob and put some distance between myself and the slower women. I settled back into a brisk walk toward the end of the airfield, grateful for the shaded path the route took into a grove of trees. The fragrant smell of jasmine filled the air and I breathed it in deeply, energized by its intoxicating scent.

After a while, the group dissipated and I was alone. The minutes marked on as I trudged through sandy tank trails and paved roads with no other person in sight. Periodically, a few cadre in a van would appear, driving by slowly to check on our progress. As I tramped on, the words of Joshua 1:9 replayed in my head over and over. *Be strong and courageous.* God was on my side.

The sun was getting lower in the sky by the time I reached the checkpoint with a timing mat placed across the width of the road. It didn't make sense for this to be the finish line. There was no one else around and we were in the middle of nowhere. An NCO with a clipboard called out as I approached.

"Candidate two six, continue to follow the orange cones." The timing chip on my boot chirped as I crossed the mat. I guessed that the checkpoint was at the six-mile mark and had been set up as a decoy. I shuffled along under the creaking weight of my overloaded rucksack, mile after mile. Finally, after dark the route ended back at the camp. We must have walked at least 12 miles. I was happy to see that I had finished somewhere in the middle of the pack. Candidates continued to trickle in as I sat down at a picnic table with the women who had already finished. There was food in plastic mermite containers for our dinner. I was hungry but could hardly eat. My stomach was in queasy knots from not eating for several hours and the oral rehydration salts we had been forced to drink during our march. I willed myself to eat several bites and drink two cups of sugary Kool-Aid, knowing we wouldn't eat again until morning most likely.

Over the next five days we were challenged to the edges of our physical and mental capacities. We spent each day with our rucksacks strapped to our backs, walking all over remote training areas. At night we sat on metal chairs and wrote essays on a variety of assigned topics, delirious from less than three hours of sleep each night. Our eager runs back and forth between the tents and the whiteboard for instructions quickly turned into awkward shuffles. Blisters and intense soreness caught up with even the most physically fit. By the end of the week we looked like a pathetic hoard of zombies, lurching over the rocks in an attempt to feign running.

As much pain as our bodies were in that week, from blisters on top of blisters, raw shoulders and hipbones and cramped muscles, we still managed to turn mutual suffering into bonding. We laughed over our mutual suffering and feelings of ineptitude when we were asked to perform complex tasks with very little guidance under the fog of sleep deprivation. The women encouraged one another and looked after their small tribe as we navigated the unknown to the surprise of the cadre. They were constantly emphasizing that helping our buddies out would be of no personal benefit to us, but we formed tight bonds and refused to leave any straggler behind.

The women I met amazed me. They were the cream of the crop soldiers coming from every background and skill set, from elite all-Army athletes to helicopter pilots and a former Olympian. Each candidate was strong, smart and fiercely determined. I had never been in the company of so many talented and strong women during my time in the Army and felt privileged to be in their midst. We seemed to all want the same thing – to break free of the traditional career path and forge a new path forward for women in combat.

On the final day of selection 3rd Squad dragged weary bodies out across the rocks with our loaded rucksacks, feeling every blister and sore muscle under the weight of our packs. It was 3:00 a.m., and we had slept for only a couple hours after writing essays all night. We waited for instructions, speculating what brutal challenges the final day would bring.

"Follow the orange cones…" an NCO with a clipboard began. We knew the drill. Walk until someone gives you other instructions. Do what you're told. Don't talk to anyone else.

By the time the sun broke the horizon we were drained and sweat-soaked. The morning had been brutally hard. Most of it involved carrying several hundred pounds of equipment between our team members along with our heavy rucksacks and weapons. After that particularly brutal challenge was over, we carried our team-mates, one or two at a time, along the sandy tank trails of backwoods Fort Bragg, lost in an endless maze of pine trees and zig-zagging roads, all the while trying to remember constantly changing series of numbers given to us individually by the cadre to test our memory. We were all digging deep into our physical and mental reserves to continue putting one foot in front of the other with any dignity.

We stopped at a fork in the road sometime before noon, where a sandy tank trail split off from the rough gravel main road, and cadre ordered us to drop our rucksacks. They announced it was time for an unknown time and distance run. Uniform pants, t-shirt, running shoes and utility vests with canteens attached was the uniform for the event. I slid my heavy rucksack off my shoulder onto the ground with a *thump* and began to unzip my sweat-soaked uniform top. I did a double take as I realized there were bright pink spots underneath my front chest pockets. I looked down at my rucksack straps, puzzled. They were damp and pink on the undersides. As I unzipped my jacket and removed it, an embarrassing realization sunk in – the dye from my brand new hot pink sports bra had stained my t-shirt and jacket. It was the first time I had worn it, and the heat plus my excessive sweat created perfect conditions for it to bleed right through my clothes. My light tan t-shirt was highlighter pink from my collarbone to my belly button. There was no hiding it.

The group of all-male cadre snickered quietly behind their clipboards, trying not to break character, as I sat down to tie my running shoes. My cheeks were hot with mortification. Of all times and places for me to have a major faux pas, did it have to be in front of a bunch of special operations guys when I was trying my hardest to be taken seriously? I cringed inwardly and took to the starting line, grateful for the vest that partially obscured my neon pink shirt.

Back at Fort Bragg the cadre dismissed us for a few hours while they made the final decision on who made the cut. Third squad decided on IHOP for a post-selection feast. We were still crusted with sweat and filth from the week, but none of us cared – we were ravenous. We piled into two cars in our cleanest uniforms and navigated our way to downtown Fayetteville where we laughed and fretted over mounds of chocolate chip pancakes, bacon and eggs, wondering who was going to make it.

Back on post we stood anxiously outside a large classroom, waiting to be called in to find out our fates. The women who went in didn't come back out, but were shuttled outside through one of two doors, the *selects* kept separate from the *non-selects*. We chattered nervously, waiting to hear our names.

"Lieutenant Morris," the Staff. Sgt. in charge of us ushered me to a small table inside the room. I sat down in front of the female NCO across from me and swallowed hard.

"Ma'am, you need to work on your interpersonal skills and your physical fitness," she read off the sheet in front of her. "Otherwise, your performance was fine. Congratulations, you've been selected. Do you have any questions for me?" I shook my head, which buzzed with a fuzzy cocktail of adrenaline and sleep deprivation. The NCO gestured me to a door on the far side of the room. I burst out of the frigid air-conditioned room into the muggy afternoon. A group of other "selects" yelled and cheered as I walked out. Leah was there and a couple of third squad women, too. I joined in cheering for the rest of the women who walked out the door. There were 31 of us, whittled down from a starting group of 56.

The cadre came out and addressed us, calling off five names from a clipboard and asking us to stand aside. My heart raced when I heard my name called, hoping there hadn't been some sort of mistake in the selection announcements.

"Ladies, we can only take 26 of you for the summer training and deployment," the Major announced as my heart sank into my boots. "The other five of you will attend a training course in October and deploy after the New Year." He turned and ushered the remaining 26 women onto a waiting bus with their bags. They would drive overnight to Georgia to get outfitted with new gear and complete their training before heading to Afghanistan in August.

My heart absolutely broke as I watched the other women get on the bus, hugging and laughing as they started their new adventure. I thought I would be with them. Now I would have to return to my unit, to my thankless staff job and my boss with his weird cryptic sayings and awkward hand gestures. I had already packed up part of my apartment in anticipation for getting selected. Suddenly, I felt foolish.

The five of us and all the *non-selects* returned to the Landmark Inn with our bags. The front desk handed me a freshly baked chocolate chip cookie and a piece of paper with my flight information on it. My flight left the following day. We each got our own rooms that night, and I was grateful for the privacy. As the room door swung open, I dropped my bags on the floor and began crying. It felt almost like I hadn't been selected. I knew I was being a baby, but in my exhaustion I couldn't do anything but let the tears flow freely. After a few minutes, my eyes settled on the phone sitting on the nightstand. I dialed my parents' home number from the room phone and my mom picked up.

"Hi mama, I got selected!" I said, choking back the disappointment in my voice.

"Well congratulations, sweetheart! We're so proud of you!" she replied excitedly, calling my dad over and putting me on speakerphone. I explained the delay in training and deployment to my parents, bursting into tears again over my small heartbreak.

"You know, there's a reason for that," my mom said assuredly. "God has a plan in it all, you'll see."

Chapter 9

A New Family

For the next five months I eagerly chomped at the bit to get out of my unit and get to CST training. I hadn't planned on coming back after selection, so the reality of having to face the daily chaos of life in an infantry brigade again was deflating. My previous position had already been filled by one of my peers, so in the interim I was given perhaps the most loathsome job in the Army – battalion supply officer, also known as the S4 in military speak. The brigade was on the fast track to another Afghanistan deployment, so I was kept on my toes prepping the unit's equipment and vehicles to get shipped overseas and going to field training exercises in the desert of Yakima, Washington. As disappointed as I was to not be training and deploying with the girls I had gone through selection with, the five months working back at my unit ended up being what I needed.

Two weeks after returning home I found out that I had fractured my foot during selection and it needed time to heal. In the meantime, I had a great new boss, a stellar team of enlisted men and women working for me and found purpose in my work, as tedious as it was. Nevertheless, when October finally rolled around, I was ready to go.

With the help of friends, I packed all my belongings into a storage unit and said my goodbyes. My beloved Twentysomethings family at church sent me away with prayer, a card full of encouraging words and a bouquet of flowers, which made the trip across country in my front seat. It was never very hard for me to leave my friends, and I couldn't really figure out why. Moving at full speed into the next adventure was fun and exciting, even if it meant never being able to put down roots. As long as I was never the one being left behind, I was fine with the unpredictability of military life.

I left enough time in my schedule to stop at my parents' house in Illinois for a couple days on the way to North Carolina. It was nice to have home cooked food and a comfortable bed after spending three days on the road. My parents had moved away from our small hometown after I graduated from college, but their house still contained all our childhood artifacts collected over the years and familiar furniture. It felt like home enough to me. I went to bed early after I arrived for a much-needed sound night's sleep.

I woke up to daylight in the guest bedroom the next morning, October 24, and lazily grabbed my phone to surf Facebook before getting out of bed. I began to scroll through my news feed and immediately saw to my horror that it was filled with Department of Defense releases announcing that Army First Lt. Ashley White had been killed in the early hours of the morning on October 22 in Kandahar Province, Afghanistan, while supporting Army Rangers as a CST. Two Rangers, Sgt. 1st Class Kristoffer Domeij and Pvt. 1st Class Christopher Horns were also killed alongside her. One of the most unforgiving of weapons, a buried Improvised Explosive Device claimed their lives during a nighttime operation. Many friends I had gone through selection with were in Afghanistan, mourning the loss of a sister while having no option to stop and grieve. The missions continued on. I couldn't imagine the weight of the loss that they felt, nor the realization that they had several more months in a combat zone to square up to.

The news of her death felt like a knife in my heart and sent an icy feeling into the pit of my stomach. Finally, the gravity of the mission I was about to be a part of sank in. I feared for my life in a way that I hadn't previously. Ashley's death felt personal and eerily close. Why had I thought that because we were going to be working with the "best of the best" that we would be any safer in a combat zone? Working with elite forces meant we were going to be in the thick of the fight, whether or not politicians and military hot shots wanted women in combat or not. I felt truly scared for what was to come.

I propped myself up in bed with a pillow and shed quiet tears for Ashley, for her family and for my sisters in arms who were hurting. After a few moments I opened my one-year Bible to the reading for the day. The Old Testament passage was from Jeremiah, and I wasn't too captivated by the hellfire and damnation messages at that moment. But suddenly, I found myself catching my breath, as if someone had suddenly shouted the words I was reading right into my ears.

Because you trusted me, I will give you your life as a reward. I will rescue you and keep you safe. I, the Lord, have spoken[10].

In that moment, there was no doubt in my mind that God Himself had spoken those words of safety directly into my troubled heart. I knew without question He would bring me back from Afghanistan alive. The fear and dread I had felt only moments earlier completely dissipated.

Monday morning I was set to leave. I said goodbye to my parents the night prior, knowing they would be up early before me to go to work. I found a note from my mom on the kitchen table, propped up against the salt and pepper shakers. Since my sisters and I were kids, she was always leaving us notes on the kitchen table, giving us instructions for chores on the back of an envelope or wishing us happy birthday on a napkin in her signature cursive script.

Go with God, Meredith! I believe that you are where He wants you to be. This seems right for you. Let us know how things are going!!! See you for Christmas!! Love, Mom

I smiled and picked up the note, folding it and putting it in my bag.

I checked into the Landmark Inn on Fort Bragg and found my room, dumping my gear on one of the two queen beds. For the next six weeks I would be a student at the Cultural Support Team Training Course along with 59 other women. On the first day of class the five of us who had been pushed over from the May selection found each other and rehashed the more brutal and hysterical moments of our week in the back woods of Fort Bragg the past spring. There was Alex, a charismatic leader with the itinerant heart of a poet. Sam, who had been a part of my squad at selection, was the most physically strong woman I had ever met, with a deep well of artistic talent and rock-steady nerves.

---

10 Jeremiah 39:18

Keesha possessed equal parts pensiveness and attitude and could disarm you with a thoughtful word and a dramatic eye roll. Camille, a brainy veterinarian with a wicked sense of humor and heart for adventure rounded out our crew.

Over the weeks, the five of us became a family of sorts inside our class. Alex humorously bestowed titles on each of us. Sam and Camille, the more mature of the five of us, were dad and mom, respectively. Keesha and I were sisters, and Alex gamely took on the title of little brother. On weekends off we gallivanted around Fayetteville, North Carolina and Savannah, Georgia, eating, taking in the sights and spectating at Alex's rugby tournaments. I went to rural North Carolina with Camille over Thanksgiving to meet some of her relatives and enjoy a small-town bluegrass concert in the local bingo hall. We made the most of our newfound sisterhood over the course of three months and gained true lifelong friends in each other.

The training course itself was a mix of classroom lectures and discussions, intense physical and mental training and practical field exercises. A revolving door of instructors came and went each day, imparting their wisdom on a variety of subjects from Afghan culture and history to Village Stability Operations doctrine and how to build rapport. The Cultural Support Team program was created by the special operations community to meet a desperate need on the battlefield. Because of cultural restraints in Afghanistan male coalition forces had no access to the female portion of the population. Afghan women were generally kept at home out of the public eye and could not interact with men who weren't their family members. Special operations units realized they were missing a large piece of the puzzle by not being able to interact with the local women. Women were the eyes and ears of the village and the hub of the Afghan household. The CST program would help fill in the missing piece of the puzzle. A well-trained CST could provide services that range from searching women for weapons and gathering critical operational information to building rapport and facilitating trust in the local government. Still, there were no hard and fast rules about how Cultural Support Teams were supposed to operate in Afghanistan and what the integration of women into Ranger and Special Forces units would look like. They were figuring it out as they went.

The task ahead was critically important, but many of the special operations fighters on ground had yet to see the value of working alongside women in combat. A deep culture of skepticism and misogyny was prevalent in the all-male units. Many wanted to retain the integrity of their *men-only* teams, believing whole-heartedly that women were too emotional and weak to be anything other than a liability on the battlefield. Meanwhile, Ashley White's death launched a polarizing debate about the role of women in combat. It became increasingly challenging to have a productive conversation about the value of women on the frontlines.

Time and time again the cadre reminded us of our inferiority as women working with elite operators. *They will not trust you until you prove your worth to them. You must find a way to be useful outside of doing your job – help out around camp. Don't be a distraction. Don't sleep with the team guys. Be valuable. Prove yourself worthy.* The rhetoric was continuous and irritating and by the end of the course I felt anxious about going down range. The parameters of the Cultural Support Team duties were still in the gray area and our every move was under intense scrutiny.

One sleepy afternoon during a particularly painful lecture, a male Staff Sergeant suddenly burst into our classroom and told us to get out immediately – he had reserved our classroom for the afternoon and we needed to find another place to hold our session. Our instructor, a female Sergeant First Class, stood her ground as he became increasingly angry that we weren't vacating our seats. The 60 of us watched wide-eyed as the Staff Sgt. berated our instructor, who calmly explained that we were CST women in the middle of training.

"CST? Does that stand for cooking and sewing team? Don't you guys just sit around and drink tea?" he fired at her. "Women don't belong in combat. I can't believe you're training them for this b***s*** mission." We gasped in unison and several women began to jump to our instructor's defense. He continued on belligerently for several tense minutes before suddenly bursting out laughing. Our instructor also began to laugh as we stared confusingly at them, wondering what had just taken place. It had all been a staged joke, apparently, to show us what we could be up against. Several of the women sighed or chuckled in relief, but most of them, including myself, didn't find the joke funny.

At the end of the course we traveled back out to Camp Mackall for the culminating exercise that would put our newfound skills to the test. The weeklong exercise would simulate deployment conditions. We would operate out of a makeshift Forward Operating Base and patrol into mock villages populated with Pashto and Arabic-speaking male and female actors. It was early December, and the nighttime temperatures dropped below freezing each night. The unheated tents were miserable. I shivered in my cot each night, bundled in long underwear and my physical training jacket and pants. I was grateful for the long early morning patrols and the chance to get my blood pumping after a fitful night's rest. In teams, we navigated to different missions, taking turns to conduct cultural engagements in groups of three while the cadre evaluated our performances.

By the end of the course the cadre whittled us down to an even smaller group of 40-some. Several women had been cut during the training for not meeting standards, and others made it through the entire training course to discover they had not been selected to deploy as a CST. Some of the women would be assigned to work with Rangers in Afghanistan, and some with Special Forces. The Rangers were the so-called *door kickers,* preferring to move under the cover of night, disappearing before the sun rose and conducting operations on high value targets. Special Forces, though no less tactically proficient, were heavily invested in Village Stability Operations in Afghanistan, which involved training local government and military forces, establishing security from the ground up. During the final week we received our assignments. I would be working with Special Forces along with Camille. Alex and Keesha would deploy with the Rangers, and Sam was assigned to a Navy SEAL team.

With the Green Berets, we would live and work out of austere camps called Village Stability Platforms. The VSPs were located inside villages where the teams would live and work alongside their Afghan Partners. It didn't sound like a glamorous mission, but I wanted to do something that involved creative thinking and building relationships. The idea of working with Rangers on direct action missions sounded exciting, but I knew it wasn't my style of work. I would be content finding unconventional solutions to unconventional problems and drinking *a lot* of tea with the locals.

Special Forces had transitioned to Village Stability Operations over the previous two years, rather than traditional "insurgent hunting." This relatively new methodology was based in four basic principles: 1. *Shape*. Permissively imbed in local villages and earn the trust of local governance. 2. *Hold*. Secure and protect the village against immediate threats and continue to gain trust. 3. *Build*. From the bottom up, reinforce local government, build up Afghan security forces and equip the people. 4. *Transition*. We wouldn't be in Afghanistan forever, so we had a responsibility to educate and empower the people to secure themselves for the long term.

Though the steps seem simple enough, the VSO mission was ambiguous, constantly changing and required creativity and flexibility from village to village. One answer to a problem in a village in the South is bound to be radically different from a village in the North. What CSTs were tasked to do, as Special Operations Forces enablers, is provide another line of communication to a previously inaccessible portion of the population: women. As CST members, we weren't going to empower the women, promote women's rights or host any burka-burning parties. Our purpose was to facilitate operations by building relationships with the local people, gathering information and influencing the women (as well as men and children) to promote long-term stability. What this war was all about was fighting for influence. The people of Afghanistan held the keys to their own future, and we were simply going to be facilitators in training their local security and armed forces to render the Taliban ineffective, in theory.

My best friend, Ann, now an Army nurse stationed at Fort Bragg, came to the Cultural Support Team graduation ceremony just before Christmas. Our friendship had endured four years of post-college Army life, with all its ups and downs. Even though we had only seen each other a handful of times since graduating I knew she was always cheering me on from afar. After eating lunch with her I packed up my car and made the long drive home to Illinois for Christmas.

Chapter 10

Pinholes

With the New Year came new adventures. I thought back on the events of 2011, and the fact that the end of the previous year, I was bitter, stuck and frustrated, spending the first half of 2010 in a combat zone, and the second half doing damage control, trying to get my mind and body back to a healthy, positive state. My only goal going into 2011, which I warily set for myself was *more*. I wanted something more significant out of my life: more challenges, more adventure, just *more*. I couldn't really articulate what it was that I needed, I just knew there was some ache in my heart that yearned for a fuller life.

Oswald Chambers relates life's seemingly inconsequential series of events to tiny pinholes.

"My personal life may be crowded with small, petty happenings, altogether insignificant. But if I obey Jesus Christ in the seemingly random circumstances of life, they become pinholes through which I see the face of God."

When looked at from far away, pinholes don't look like much of anything. You can't see through the tiny openings unless you're up close. But when you peer through them at a close distance, they expose a greater perspective and allow us to see through the obstacle in front of us to the world beyond. Sometimes we have to wait a while before the pinholes make sense to us. Sometimes it takes a year.

Early into 2011 I had my sights set on playing All-Army basketball. It seemed like an ideal opportunity to get *more* out of my life. I turned in my application to try out, put together a co-ed post intramural league to gain some credibility and hone my skills, and then I waited. Some time passed, and I was not asked to try out for the team. I ended our post league with a dramatic concussion sealing my destiny of *not* playing contact sports for quite some time.

Soon afterwards, my coworker sent me a flyer she had seen about recruiting women for a special operations mission in Afghanistan. Instantly, it ignited something inside of me and I knew it was something worth pursuing. Without hesitating I printed the flyer and went immediately to my boss and told him I was volunteering for the program. I felt there was so much on the line, much more than the possibility of not getting selected, so I worked hard like my career depended on it.

CST Selection week was a welcome, albeit brutal taste of the Army life that I had been missing out on sitting behind my desk writing operations orders for the previous nine months. Only 31 of the 56 women that attended the assessment were selected to go on to the next phase of training. Of the 31 of us, 6 were randomly selected to complete the next phase at a later date due to class capacity. I was incredibly disappointed to be delaying my dream by five months, but in retrospect appreciate the time I had to give my body a rest and recover from the fractured foot I incurred during selection and to say goodbye to my friends.

The second phase of CST training turned out to be much different than I expected it to be, but I learned a lot about myself, made some wonderful lifelong friends and experienced more hilarity and uncontrolled chaos than I have in ages. It was exactly what my soul needed.

Those pinholes over the course of the year all pointed to a larger picture that I couldn't see in the small moments. Life was way off course from anything I could have predicted at the beginning of the year. Yet, God heard my earnest prayer and gave me *more* than I could have manufactured for myself. He had called me into something bigger than myself and set new passions into my heart.

I spent a week with my friend Crystal back in Washington, sleeping on a mattress in the floor of her guest room while I waited to report back to Fort Bragg. I had moved out of my apartment before Christmas and most everything I owned was now in storage. The CST 3 crew was set to return after the New Year for three weeks of Pre-

Mission Training before we set out for Afghanistan. I spent the days working out and reading, enjoying the rest before the hectic onset of training. One drizzly afternoon I made my way across town to a local tattoo place. I was going to get *Courage* permanently inked on the underside of my upper left arm. I wanted to remember God's commandment to be strong and courageous as I moved boldly into another new year. He had called me out into the depths of the unknown, and I was learning to trust Him and to live with heart in the face of fear, knowing He would never leave me.

Two dozen women descended on the Landmark Inn in full force, anxious and excited to get the training out of the way and find out our location assignments. We would operate in teams of two, with each team being assigned a female interpreter. The cadre let us choose our teammates, as long as each enlisted woman had an officer teammate. Due to the surplus of officers in our group, several of us had to pair up together, captains with lieutenants to maintain some sort of rank hierarchy.

A young 1st Lieutenant named Haley was one of the odd officers out, so by default we ended up together. I didn't know much about her and hadn't spoken to her at all during the training course. She seemed friendly enough and perhaps a little green, having just been promoted. Haley was an Air Defense Artillery officer from Boston, and a self-declared *Masshole* who lived by the phrase *Go F*** Yourself,* which she had emblazoned on her water bottle. I saw our partnership as a chance to help mentor Haley. I had four years of experience under my belt, including a deployment, and had learned a lot of tough lessons that I was more than willing to share. This time around would be my chance at redemption; a chance to really have a successful, healthy deployment with a partner who was on my side. It would be the two of us against the world. I knew the challenges that lay ahead of us were potentially huge, but not insurmountable. Haley and I would figure it all out, together. I loved a good underdog story and wanted to see us come out on top.

After a brief stay at Landmark Inn we traveled out to a remote training area which would be our launching point for all our exercises over the next three weeks. The small, minimalist training base housed several sleep tents, porta-potties and showers. A dedicated Special

Forces ODA[11] was on hand to train us each day in everything from tactics to shooting to cultural engagement. Each morning we began the day learning the level 1 skills in the Special Operations Combatives Program. The intensive training involved fighting off an attacker in full body armor and helmet and takedown maneuvers. During the daytime we spent hours at the range, honing our shooting skills. We repeated simple drills over and over again, building muscle memory until we could do it all without thinking. We practiced casualty aid, applying tourniquets to each other and ourselves again and again until it was second nature. The ODA led us through patrolling tactics and maneuvers until we could react to fire in our sleep. In combat there would be no time to stop and think. We needed to know how to respond automatically in critical situations.

At night, after the ODA left us to our own devices, we loaded up into the rental minivans we had been assigned and sped through deserted back roads towards post, drawing looks of wonder and amazement from the gate guards as four vans full of women passed through. We would roll up to the Commissary and rush inside, buying trays of sushi, pizza and snacks before exiting as quickly as we entered, hoping our instructors wouldn't catch us out and about. Then we'd return to our austere FOB and feast on our spoils, laughing and badly singing along to the Spice Girls the entire way. Our lively camaraderie helped us thrive throughout the three otherwise challenging weeks of training.

On February 16, 2012 we arrived at the passenger terminal with our gear several hours before our flight to Germany on a cool rainy morning. Several of the CST women assigned to the Ranger units were there to see us off along with an assortment of family members and friends. While we were waiting in the passenger terminal for our plane, our team Physician Assistant, Debra, gave us each a rabies vaccination in the women's bathroom. She instructed us to line up and drop our

---

[11] Operational Detachment-Alpha, a 12-man team of Green Berets

pants for the shot, which sent us into a fit of hysteria at the ridiculousness of the situation. It was unorthodox, but necessary pre-deployment preparation.

Finally, after what seemed like an eternity, it was time to load the plane. We walked single file out to the waiting tail ramp of the aircraft and climbed on board the waiting C-17. It was really happening now. Everything I had worked so hard for was laid before me. God had brought me so far, leading me into a great adventure that I could hardly have dreamed of a year earlier.

Chapter 11

Back to the Beginning

We spread out in the belly of the massive C-17, rolling out sleeping bags and blankets in the aisle, attempting to get comfortable for the nine-hour flight to Ramstein Air Base. Gratefully, there weren't many of us on the flight so we each got an inward-facing seat along the side of the plane. Giant pallets of our duffle bags and tough boxes filled the main cargo area between the rows of seats. I placed my assault pack on the floor in front of my seat and stretched my legs out on top of it. It was cold and drafty towards the rear of the plane where I was sitting, so I tugged my fleece cap on and wrapped up in my insulated poncho liner. Now *this* was the way to fly into a combat zone. I popped a Dramamine tablet and dozed off before we even left the runway. The next nine hours passed relatively quickly in a sleepy haze. We spent the night at Ramstein Air Base, waiting for the next open flight into Afghanistan early the following morning.

At last we arrived bleary eyed at Bagram Airfield, a large NATO base in northeastern Afghanistan. BAF, for short, was the home of the Special Operations Task Force-Afghanistan, the headquarters which oversaw all special operations in the country. We would meet the outgoing CSTs there and receive debriefs from the teams about our operating areas. Haley and I knew that we were tentatively assigned to Zabul Province, where we would replace the CST working with a team of Green Berets. After a long, cramped bus ride across the base, the CST manager, Rebecca, led us into a massive circus-style tent filled with dozens of bunks. We would stay there the next three weeks while we transitioned with the outgoing women.

Sleepily, we claimed our bunks and crashed for the next several hours. The outgoing CST 2 women were still arriving from their sites in Afghanistan and wouldn't be all together for a few more days. Until then, we had time to recover from jet lag and get our bearings. I fell sound asleep inside my sleeping bag and slept for hours straight, unaware of the passage of time. I woke up fuzzy-brained in the late afternoon with a sick stomach, and immediately regretted taking my malaria prophylactic on an empty stomach.

The next day we met Alexa and Brynne, the women Haley and I were replacing in Zabul Province. Their interpreter, Fatima, was with them. She would go back to the VSP with us for the remainder of our deployment. Fatima was young, barely 26 years old, and had left behind two children and a husband in Michigan to provide her language services to U.S. Special Forces. Fatima had an Afghan mother and a Pakistani father, both Pashtuns, and spoke several languages fluently. She would be a huge asset to our mission.

We spent three tortuously long weeks at BAF, waiting for the green light to push out to our respective Village Stability Platforms. Shortly after we arrived in Afghanistan, coalition service members on the base mishandled a Quran, unknowingly burning it along with some of the base's garbage. News spread quickly from the local civilian contractors who worked at the incinerator. It caused an outcry across the country, and insurgents pummeled the perimeter of BAF with artillery and weapons fire, lobbing mortars directly into the base during hours of darkness. Water and food resupplies were cut off for several days and operations came to a standstill temporarily.

To non-Muslims, the incident may have seemed overblown, with a disproportional amount of backlash taken against Americans. However, Islam is so deeply and intricately woven into the Afghan culture, that there really is no greater offense any individual could commit against their way of life than to mishandle their holy books. Unfortunately, the incident, which was the result of an oversight on coalition forces' part, caused significant outbreaks of increased hostility across the country, including two Army officers being shot and killed in Kabul. We were all chomping at the bit to get to work, albeit wary of the current volatility of the situation we were going into. Though spring and summer seemed like faraway dreams in the ice-covered world of Bagram, we were all too aware of what the warmer weather would soon bring – fighting season. Taliban insurgents hole up in Pakistan for the winter while the mountain passes are closed with snow, then come crawling back out of the mountains into Afghanistan to greet the forces on the ground with their arsenal of weapons, from grenades and AK-47s, to IEDs and suicide vests. Before we left, we each had our picture taken in front of a flag-draped wall, a sobering reminder of the hostilities we could potentially face. In the event of our death, that would be the photo of us the world would see.

⛰

At last, Haley, Fatima and I got a flight into Kandahar Airfield. From there we would catch another flight into the VSP in Zabul. Kandahar was warm and sunny, a welcome contrast to snowy Bagram. Haley and I stayed on the small Special Forces compound while we waited for our flight into Zabul Province. Two other CST women, Gretchen and Carly, stayed with us, waiting for transportation into a remote area of Kandahar Province. We occupied a small wooden building outfitted with cots, which served as transient quarters for us and our two interpreters in the meantime. With little to do besides check the flight schedule once a day, we passed the time by working out twice a day and exploring the Boardwalk. Even Fatima joined in our workouts, learning how to do deadlifts and pull-ups. She would flex her biceps and smile, asking if she looked any stronger than yesterday.

I loved having Gretchen and Carly around. They were both wild and endearing and had become my good friends during training. Haley and I still hadn't bonded, despite our close proximity and my attempts to get to know her better. A small thread of tension existed between us, but I couldn't quite put my finger on it. Haley wasn't unpleasant or unkind, but something just didn't feel right. I shrugged it off, figuring we would have plenty of time to get to know each other when we got to our VSP.

One hot afternoon Haley, Gretchen, Carly and I put on our body armor and boots and decided to take a walk through the dusty back roads of KAF for a workout. As we came around a bend along the southern fence line, I immediately recognized my old brigade's former footprint. The A Company command post, with its wooden porch and tin roof, was still standing, occupied by another Stryker brigade.

"That's where my commander used to scream at me!" I pointed

92

out to the other women. So many memories came flooding back as we walked through the gravel motor pool where the BSB had staged for its convoys. It was strange and surreal to be back on KAF less than two years later. So much had changed since I saw it last, yet so much was still the same. I hadn't expected to ever see that place again after I left in June 2010. The back fence overlooking Tarnac Farms, a former Al-Qaeda training camp, was the same, as was the pervasive heavy smell of human waste from the Poo Pond. The Boardwalk, once a small collection of shops built around a sandy courtyard, had turned into a strange paradise in the middle of the desert. There was a TGI Fridays restaurant and a pizza place, which provided salsa dancing in the evenings. Someone had built a running track in the courtyard along with a large outdoor hockey rink emblazoned with a red Canadian maple leaf. In 2010 the Boardwalk, named for the wooden walkway connecting the businesses, was nothing more than a few souvenir shops, a shawarma stand and a t-shirt printing place.

One morning at breakfast inside the compound Haley and I met a tall Green Beret named Tom. He had come from the VSP that Haley and I were on our way to. He made trips back to KAF regularly to pick up supplies for the resident ODA and would fly back with us, whenever there was a flight to Zabul. Tom was kind and straightforward and did his best to prepare us for life at the VSP. The team wasn't thrilled about the presence of women at their camp, but there were ways for Haley and I to work and be successful. He thought the world of his team but acknowledged they might be a little difficult to deal with.

I writhed under the prospect of the monumental task ahead of us, of building trust with a group of elite Green Berets and proving that we had something to offer them. Haley and I wouldn't really know how we were going to contribute to the team until got to the VSP and started working. We would figure out everything as we went along. The nervous feeling in my stomach I'd carried with me for the last month and a half never quite went away as we waited two weeks at KAF for a flight. I wished I could fast forward to a month or so later. I always hated the beginning of something new – the *breaking* in phase. Being already in the groove and routine of life was more enjoyable. Beginnings made me nervous. I could never sleep the night before the first day of school as a kid. Meeting new people was terrible but loved having old friends. Familiarity was my sweet spot. I hoped and prayed I had what it took to meet the challenge head on.

Finally, we had a flight out. It was time to get to work.

Mom and dad pinning on my gold 2nd Lt. bars in 2008

On a C-17 aircraft flying into Kandahar Airfield, Afghanistan, 2009

The slow, perilous trek across the desert to Sangin, Afghanistan,
2010

Weapons practice on the range while stranded in Sangin, 2010

Promotion to Captain, 2011

Our CST family at Alex's rugby game L-R Camille, Sam, Keesha
and Alex, 2011

Air drop of food and supplies in Shajoy, Afghanistan, 2012

With Schester outside our bunker home in Sar Howza, 2012

Visiting a girls school in Sar Howza with Lynn, 2012

Celebrating Eid with Special Squad and the ODA, 2012

With Tyler on our wedding day on Waikiki Beach, Oahu, 2014

Chapter 12

Neverland

The Chinook banked and I could see blue snowcapped mountains out the back trail. The view was breathtaking, and at the same time, made me feel so small and isolated. I wasn't exactly sure where in Zabul province we were going. Haley and I had been briefed the name of the Village Stability Platform we were assigned to, but we weren't quite sure where it was. I had been to various parts of the province during my first deployment while running logistical convoys and couldn't help but wonder where we were in relation to my old stomping grounds. The helicopter finally touched ground on a landing pad a couple hundred yards from a small compound surrounded by concertina wire and Hesco barriers. A ridge of mountains jutted up imposingly behind us, and the expanse of a sprawling mud village lay beyond the compound. Haley, Fatima and I hastily exited the Chinook with our gear in tow.

Suddenly, a vivid memory flooded my mind. The haunting realization sank in that I was in the heart of Shajoy District, the same place I had been in 2009[12]. I could visualize those same mountains silhouetted against the night sky, lit up by illumination rounds fired by Army infantry troops hunting Taliban on the backside of the ridge. We were standing only yards away from where my soldiers and I had been left stranded with Maj. Rodriguez's broken vehicle, subject to a long night of mishaps. I had watched the sun rise eerily over the same mud village while the call to prayer played over loudspeakers at the local mosque. The strange coincidence gave me chills, but I had little time to dwell on it.

---

[12] COP Sangar, the former home of the infantry company that led the mission that night, was visible from the VSP

A ragtag group of men on ATVs wearing an amusing jumble of military issue and civilian clothes roared out of the entry point to the compound and overtook us. There was no conversation – the roar of the helicopter taking off was too loud. In a flash they loaded our bags and tough boxes onto the ATVs and beckoned us to jump on. I had the immediate impression that I was in the company of Peter Pan and his lost boys, not an elite team of Army Green Berets. Underneath their baseball caps the men had wild hair and outgrown beards, products of several months of relaxed grooming standards. More than one man was bizarrely sporting a pair of bubblegum pink Croc slip-ons. They had various weapons and knives strapped to their belts and looked like a little tribe of unsupervised, overgrown kids. They whipped and sped their way to the compound on the ATVs through deep mud, whooping and laughing. Haley, Fatima and I were bewildered and white knuckled, in tow.

After pulling into the compound, which would be our home for the next 9 months, we met the ODA team leader, a young captain named Aaron. A few of the guys who had picked us up from the landing zone showed us around. If I didn't think we were in Neverland before, it sure felt like it then. The indoor structures in the compound were mostly Afghan mud and straw with tiny, low doorways. By all appearances, the builder had no real blueprint when he constructed the facilities and added little rooms here and there wherever he felt like it. Ladders and narrow stairs lead to rooftops and tucked away sleeping quarters. Low archways in outdoor walls supplied continuous hazards. Stones and wooden pallets served as walkways through the deep mud, which seemed to cover every bit of ground. American-constructed plywood rooms and military-issue tents rounded out the hodgepodge of hideaways in the small camp.

The room Haley, Fatima and I were to share was a small plywood building next to the operations center. There was enough room inside for four makeshift beds, built of plywood and cheap mattresses at varying heights and sizes to accommodate the small quarters. Tom had mentioned that there was another female on the base who would be living with us, an intelligence specialist named Megan, but we had yet to meet her. It would be a tight squeeze with four of us together.

Haley and I spent the first few hours in our new home

attempting to settle in and unpack. Dried mud covered the cheap rug on the plywood floor and a layer of fine dust covered everything else. There was hardly any space for our gear, so we ended up leaving most of it in our tough boxes. We were literally living on top of each other. I claimed the bottom bunk, which was really just a cot with a mattress on top of it, nestled tightly under Haley's chest-height plywood bed. I made a mental note to not sit up too quickly while lying down. Fatima had a low bed in the far corner, and Megan's elevated bed was directly across from the door.

It was mid-March when we arrived, which meant it was still decidedly winter at 6,500 feet elevation. The worn-out Chigo heating unit on the wall in our room struggled to keep the room at a cool 59 degrees during the day. I was grateful to find that the previous CST had left us each an electric blanket for the cold nights. I dug my cheap Target sheets and fleece blanket out of my tough box and made up my bed, trying to will my small space to feel homey. Haley hung a string of Christmas lights over her bed, which she plugged into the suspicious looking Chinese-inscribed transfer box[13] in the room.

Moments later, the wooden door swung open and our fourth roommate, Megan, entered. Much to my surprise I immediately recognized her – she was one of the candidates that had not been chosen at the same CST selection I had gone through. She already worked in the Special Forces community, a fact that was well known amongst the cadre and candidates at selection the previous May. I remember Megan had wept bitterly after being told she wasn't right for the CST mission. And here Haley and I were, in her home, doing the job that she had wanted so badly to do. At first Megan didn't recognize me, but after I jogged her memory of our past encounter as gently as possible, her face noticeably fell. I introduced Haley, somewhat embarrassed, and tried with little avail to cut the tension with friendly chitchat. I felt bad that our presence was going to be a painful reminder for her, but there wasn't much we could do to change our circumstances.

Later that evening we had a chance to meet the entire team of Green Berets and the rest of the support personnel living on the VSP.

---

[13] Suspicions were correct – the box eventually caught fire and ruined Haley's Christmas lights

Haley and I found out very quickly that we were not a welcome presence to some of the men. As Aaron introduced his team and we said a few words of greeting, one man on the team, known affectionately by his teammates as "Gramps," refused to make eye contact or speak to us. At best, the rest of the team appeared indifferent to our presence. We also met the rest of the U.S. support personnel on the base. Anyone who wasn't a Green Beret earned the title of *enabler*. Our sole purpose was to support the ODA's mission with our specific talents. A Navy combat cameraman (Sean), an Air Force tactical air controller (Jake), a cook (Brad), a generator mechanic (Marcus), a canine handler and his dog (Ben and Hank, respectively), and a satellite mechanic (Darren), and two psychological operations specialists (Andy and Garret) rounded out the rest of the underdog cast of military enablers on the camp.

After that first meeting I knew it would take time and effort on our part to build rapport with the ODA and prove that our CST could be a valuable asset to their mission. We had been told more than once during training to practice building rapport with the men we were going to be working with by pulling our weight around camp and finding ways to be useful. The phrases *prove your worth, be of value* and *measurable success* were etched in our psyche, giving us inferiority complexes from the outset. We had also been repeatedly told as we were entering our respective deployments that the cards were not stacked in our favor. It wasn't a secret that many men working in special operations didn't want women working with them, and women in combat were currently at the center of a polarizing debate. At best, many saw us as distractions – at worst, liabilities. Our trainers told us to work hard and to not expect to be liked. I wasn't unfamiliar with the struggles of being an unwelcome underdog and hoped that I could prove myself to be a competent, hardworking officer. If I could win over Maj. Rodriguez, then surely I could earn the respect of the team.

The first night at the VSP Haley and I settled into our bunks under our hand-me-down electric blankets. It was below freezing outside and the wall heater periodically turned off in its struggle to produce heat inside the un-insulated room. A few hours after we went to bed I woke up in a panic, disoriented by the total darkness and unfamiliar surroundings. I fumbled for the headlamp under my pillow and turned it on long enough to get my bearings and not awaken my roommates. As I willed my fluttering heart rate to return to normal, a wave of crushing loneliness hit me hard. We were so far out in the middle of nowhere, and 'safety' was now a relative term. There was no comfort of being on a large base with ample security measures. The closest U.S. forces were a 90-minute drive away. My family and friends were 7,000 miles away and may as well have been on a different planet. Our whole world was now contained within the mud walls of the small compound.

In the dark I found myself wondering anxiously if I was going to be happy working there. Would I get to know and trust the people and vice versa? Would our CST really find purposeful work? Do we have what it takes to be *measurably successful*? Only time would tell. I took a deep breath and prayed for the strength and competency to make the most of the next several months. I recalled a few weeks earlier what I had read from 1 Peter in my daily Bible reading. *"So be truly glad. There is wonderful joy ahead, even though you have to endure many trials for a little while."* I felt God remind me that I am never alone; that He had gone before me and goes with me and behind me to make a way for me. I knew in that moment I was not forsaken and not without purpose. A warm wash of peace flooded over me, and I fell back asleep as quickly as I had awakened.

Chapter 13

Hearts and Minds

The next month and a half in Shajoy passed with only moderate rapport-building progress to report. The ODA rarely brought us along on missions, and when they did, they could only justify bringing one of us along due to space constraints. They wanted all of their "heavy hitters" on missions, and Haley and I were not high on the priority list. Most of the missions she and I were brought along on were what we considered *touchy-feely*, and involved drinking copious amounts of tea while listening to the complaints of men in the village. Haley and I rotated who went on out on mission to keep it fair. Some of the team members had warmed up to our presence, but most remained indifferent towards us. They weren't unkind, but they definitely kept their distance. Gramps still refused to acknowledge or speak to us. Megan, despite my best efforts and extending friendliness, was not interested in being friends and spent her days tucked away in a small office, only to return to our room after lights out.

Aaron joked that leading his team was like managing a professional sports team. He spent more time accommodating egos than managing actual talent. The rest of the men on the team were afraid if Haley and I went on missions that we might somehow disgrace them by being the first to kill an enemy in the event of contact. They wanted that sole honor, so we found ourselves frequently left behind. The only people at the VSP who didn't seem to be bothered by our presence were the interpreters and other enablers, the non-SF military personnel. In addition to Fatima, there were a handful of male interpreters on our base, most of them U.S. citizens and a couple Afghans who spoke both English and the local Pashto dialect.

Haley and I soon found out that Shajoy District was an incredibly conservative area of Zabul Province, being only a few hours' drive from the insurgent hotbed in Kandahar Province. In fact, most of the southern and eastern parts of the country were conservative strongholds. Women, on the occasion they were allowed to leave their homes, had to be accompanied by a male family member, and they were required to be covered head to toe in the traditional burqa. Women could not speak to men who weren't their family members, and certainly couldn't speak to foreign military men. Haley and I wanted more than anything to get access to these women – we knew they would be a valuable source of information. The Taliban had a heavy presence in Zabul and the women were the eyes and ears of the village. Very little in their family circle or community happened outside of their knowledge. We were eager to reach them, but we didn't really know how to do so if we couldn't get out of our camp regularly.

Our chain of command demanded quantifiable data from all the CSTs in Afghanistan in order to see if we were making a difference at our various locations. They tracked success by the numbers – how many engagements we had with locals, how many women we spoke with, how many radios or books or school supplies we gave out and the number of missions we went on. We were expected to report our progress daily via email and weekly via teleconference. The future of the CST program was tenuous, and all eyes were on us, from the Pentagon on down, to see what we could do. Success on our collective part would significantly sway the argument that women belonged and could succeed on the front lines. Failure could have devastating consequences for the future of women in combat.

Our core CST mission statement was ever changing, and we didn't have a solid grasp (and neither did our higher headquarters, so it seemed) on what exactly we were supposed to be doing day to day to help further Village Stability Operations in Afghanistan. We knew in broad terms what our training had equipped us to do, but we heavily relied on our own smarts and adaptability to achieve success. Additionally, we depended heavily on the favor of the teams we were working with to integrate us into their mission. When it was all said and done, they were the customers.

Between Haley and I we had an eclectic range of skills, which we determined to put to good use. She was an Air Defense officer who had studied robotics. I was a nursing school dropout with an art degree and logistics background. We were both smart and adaptable and I knew we could figure things out on the fly. We filled our downtime helping out wherever we could, mostly assisting the team's medics in the aid station on camp, where the greatest need was. Kyle and Ryan, the medics, taught us how to start IV drips, willingly offering their arms as pincushions to us for practice on. They also reviewed basic casualty care with us and checked our abilities to apply tourniquets under the pressure of time.

Nearly every day local men would bring their sick or injured children to our gate for medical care. When they arrived Kyle and Ryan would radio for Haley and I, and we would rush to our room to get Fatima and our headscarves. Even though neither of us had what anyone would consider extensive medical training, our basic skills were enough to assist the medics with whatever they needed. Our main purpose was often to help calm the small, children that found themselves on an examination table under florescent lights, being prodded by foreign men in strange uniforms.

Fatima, being a mother herself, was an invaluable presence inside the aid station. When she wasn't translating between the American medics and the locals, she was comforting the kids receiving care. We saw all kinds of injuries and illnesses pass through the rudimentary aid station, from intentional burns meant to quiet a screaming baby and farming equipment accidents, to skin diseases from poor hygiene and opium overdoses. On the very rare occasion, a woman accompanied by her husband, would come to the front gate, having heard that there were women on the camp that could provide medical care for her. The women were always small, no bigger than an average American 10-year old, but were aged severely by a hard life in rural Afghanistan. We had a list of questions that we would ask the women in order to gather their basic demographic information. But, with so little time to establish trust, the women weren't very eager to speak with us. They were generally malnourished and frail, having given birth to child after child beginning at a young age. Most of them complained of full body pain and general unhappiness. Unfortunately, with the aid station's limited supplies and medications, there was little we could do to help them.

At least once a week I would accompany Aaron and one or two

other Green Berets and a male interpreter through a locked door in our outer wall to the District Governor's compound. Small boys would yell at us in Pashto in the courtyard before scampering off.

"Staray mashay! Staray mashay[14]!" they would scream exuberantly, leaving frightened chickens and goats in their wake.

The room the group met in at the compound was small and made of mud and straw, with dirty glass windows lining one wall. The windows let in the bright afternoon sun but absolutely no fresh air. It was stifling and reeked of body odor and cigarette smoke inside. There was just enough room inside for eight to ten of us to sit cross-legged on the floor. After removing our shoes at the door, we would sit in the tiny, cushion covered room and drink tea while the governor smoked heavily and side-eyed me with disdain.

After our first visit to the compound, I understood why all the team members owned a pair of Crocs. They were easy to slip on and off before entering homes and were more durable than regular sandals. The team had inexplicably received a large shipment of only pink Crocs from an anonymous donor, which explained why several of them were sporting the bubblegum hued shoes at our arrival to the camp.

Muhammed, the district governor, was a very large, serious man, who we had nicknamed Jabba the Hut. I thought he looked vaguely like Alfred Molina in *Not without my Daughter* and was rumored to own a brothel nearby. Muhammed was not fond of my presence, but Aaron brought me along to his meetings each week in an attempt to gain the trust of some of the influential men in the community. Ultimately, Haley and I wanted to be able to access the women in the village, but our aspirations were not widely supported by the local officials. So, week after week, I sat in the insufferably hot room, praying not only for the meeting to end quickly, but that my immune system would be strong enough to overcome whatever germs I may have picked up from the questionably clean tea cup.

One week, we seemed to reach some sort of breakthrough in our meeting. Muhammed, at Aaron's request, granted me permission to address an all-male gathering at the district center in order to let them

---

14 Pashto greeting, meaning literally "may you not be tired"

know about a women's health clinic we would be hosting on the VSP. With only a few minutes notice, I had no time to prepare what I was going to say. I entered the courtyard behind Aaron and a handful of our male interpreters, where the local men were gathered for their meeting. Dozens of turban-clad men in traditional dress filled every available space in the courtyard, many sitting or squatting on the ground. Even though my head was covered out of respect, I could still feel every eye on me as I entered. The men made no effort to conceal their stares and gawked at me openly. Aaron addressed the crowd through an interpreter, then introduced me and allowed me to speak. I tried my best to not look completely embarrassed as I gave my brief message about the women's clinic, pausing several times to allow for translation. Many of the men looked away from me while I spoke, and others continued to carry on conversations with each other, obviously uninterested in anything I had to say. I left the courtyard immediately afterwards in order to allow the meeting to continue without further distraction.

On the walk back to our side of the camp, the interpreters informed me that many of the men had been making lewd jokes in Pashto while I was speaking. I was horrified but knew I would probably never see any of those men again. Whatever rapport we had built with the village men up to that point was completely blown the moment they let a blonde American woman into an all-male gathering. We all had a good laugh about it afterwards, and my mortification was eventually quelled.

When we weren't working or attempting to be helpful, Haley and I frequented what passed for a gym on the camp. A small half-domed tent served as relative protection from the elements, harboring some rusty weights and a precarious pull-up bar. It smelled faintly like a goat barn inside but was sufficient for basic strength training needs. We also participated in small group runs every few days up to a small keyhole shaped cave on the mountain ridge directly in front of our camp, gaining 400 feet of elevation over the course of the mile. The view from the top was stunning – literally breathtaking. The camp looked tiny from the high vantage point. If you squinted hard enough, the village disappeared into the desert and you could swear you weren't in one of the most dangerous places on earth. My lungs screamed every time we ran the two-mile course and never seemed to get more acclimated to the elevation. The run back down the mountain was fast and furious, if not dangerous. The steep decline, along with loose rocks and dirt were sprained ankles waiting to happen. Since we were outside of the confines of our camp, we all took turns driving one of the ATVs with our weapon alongside the runners for security. Every now and then, a curious village boy would join our pack, easily outrunning us in his cheap plastic sandals. Being able to exert myself physically kept the vague feelings of anxiety away, at least temporarily.

The camp routinely received resupplies via aircraft, as it was relatively inaccessible via local roads. Palletized boxes of food, fuel and mail from home were rigged with parachutes and dropped out of the back of U.S. Air Force C-130 planes. Depending on the pilots' schedules, we received airdrops at unpredictable, odd times. More than one occasion found us all sleepily waiting at the edge of the camp in the dark of night, listening for the sound of a distant aircraft to announce the arrival of our goods. We only had a small Bobcat forklift to help move the two-dozen or so 4'x4' boxes, so we ended up manually unpacking and carrying in most of our supplies. The whole operation from start to finish took two to three hours. We would unpack the boxes of food and immediately dig into the good snacks while we helped stack and organize dry goods in the kitchen. If there was ice cream, it was going to be a good day. We only had a small freezer for frozen goods, so the ice cream was immediately consumed. Packages from home were highly anticipated, and any containing candy or instant mac and cheese were shared throughout the camp.

On occasion during these drops the wind would pick up one of the parachuted bundles and drag it across the desert with several of us running on foot after it. Some of the parachutes never fully opened, sending bundles "burning in" at top speed to explode spectacularly on the drop zone. One morning, shortly after sunrise, the wind shifted after the bundles were halfway to the ground and sent a pallet of bottled water crashing through the roof of the compound next to the camp. We watched in horror as it knocked down part of a mud wall, realizing the family of a known Taliban commander lived there.

Several of us immediately hopped into our ATVs and hustled over to survey the damage and extricate our water from the family's

111

courtyard. The inner compound was filled with a menagerie of chickens and baby goats, seemingly unaffected by the several hundred-pound bundle that had just fallen out of the sky. Young boys excitedly flocked around us, laughing at the strange looking Americans and vying for our attention. An elderly man came out of the house and was intercepted by one of the team's interpreters, who began apologizing profusely for the accident in Pashto.

"Ask him if he wants to keep the water as an apology!" Aaron shouted.

The old man looked irritated and dismissively waved his hand towards the massive box. The conversation was brief.

The interpreter sheepishly replied, "He says no. He thinks you poisoned it."

We offered him some money to fix his wall and he readily agreed. After the transaction was made and we had loaded the box on to the Bobcat, we left as quickly as possible, laughing at our "good" fortune. The commander wasn't present and rarely returned to his home, but we were pretty sure he would hear about the incident.

Soon the fickle weather of March melted into a beautiful and clear April. It was beginning to get warmer and the periodic snow and rainstorms lessened. Most days were sunny and pleasant with cool nights. Occasionally, on clear evenings after our dinner and our daily meeting, Jake, our Air Force tactical air controller, would build a fire in the stone pit outside of the main operations center. The interpreters would bring their hookah pipes and sit around on the wooden benches, sharing pictures of their children back home and listening to traditional Afghan music played from cheap Nokia cell phones. Many of the guys on the camp weren't particularly interested in socializing, but would occasionally join in. Haley frequently excused herself under the pretense to give advanced English lessons to Farheed, one of the local interpreters that lived on the camp with us.

Chapter 14

Gaslight

As April went on, a noticeable crack began to form in the relationship between Haley and I. We had never really clicked as a pair from the outset, but I had no reason to be concerned that we wouldn't get along professionally. I noticed fairly quickly that Haley spent less and less time planning and strategizing missions with me, and more time with the team behind closed doors. She was determined to pursue her own interests and plans, which I was never privy to. Consequently, we frequently found ourselves unable to agree about the best way to support the team. The frustration of not being able to get off the camp to go into the village on missions added to our stress. We seemed to run into obstacles on every side that kept us from doing anything *measurably successful*, like we were expected to do.

I was determined to maintain the appearance of a united CST, regardless of how I felt about the current state of our partnership. More than anything, I did not want to project even the slightest appearance of discord and give the ODA more of a reason to distrust the presence of women on their camp. As the leader of the team, I felt the heavy weight of expectation on my shoulders and the responsibility to guide and direct Haley. It was entirely up to us to create our own success, together, and prove to the team that we had a unique skill that they needed for their mission. I went into the deployment with the idealistic mentality that it was going to be us against the world. Come hell or high water I had Haley's back and blindly trusted that she had mine. Our lives depended on it in a combat zone. So, I chalked up her frequently subversive behavior to immaturity and inexperience. She was young and this was her first deployment.

In my willingness to excuse Haley's behavior, I naively fell prey to her manipulation. It was subtle at first, and I didn't fully recognize the extent to which she was exploiting my emotions. I had misguidedly confided in Haley some of the struggles I had during my first deployment – how I had been in a dark place after being made a pariah by those around me that I trusted the most. Many of those same feelings of rejection and isolation had come back since being on the camp, and I told Haley I was struggling. I didn't necessarily think I could trust her with the weight of my story, but I hoped that by being vulnerable with her it could help form a bond of friendship or at the very least, empathy.

Unfortunately, my transparency gave her more fuel for the fire, and she willingly fed my insecurity. She feigned compassion for me at strategic moments to bolster my trust, and gaslighted me other times. Not long after our arrival in Shajoy, Haley began telling me that the others on the camp didn't approve of my behavior, citing my sense of humor or my interpersonal interactions with some of the team members. She interpreted every glance, comment and gesture from anyone on the camp into severe disapproval of me, and positive regard for her. Over the course of several weeks, she had me convinced that I was unprofessional, overly emotional and an ineffective leader. But in her eyes she could do no wrong, and everyone adored her. We were failing to accomplish *measurable success* as a team because of me, not for her lack of genius. Despite all of her mind games, I somehow didn't believe her to be malicious.

I truly believed that there was something wrong with how I was leading and presenting myself, so I took her corrections to heart and began to deeply doubt my abilities. I felt her accusations were confirmed by the way the other team members treated me. Most of them made it clear that they still didn't see the CST as a necessity to their mission. And they definitely weren't interested in being friends. Aaron tried his best to fit us in on missions and outreach events where he could without losing any more rapport with the male village officials or inciting discord within his own team. He was caught painfully in the middle, but ultimately his allegiance to his men and their mission won out. Being constantly slighted was disappointing, but I understood the predicament Aaron was in as a team leader.

In an effort to escape the discomfort of my daily interactions with Haley and continue my mission of being useful, I spent a lot of time in the camp kitchen helping Brad cook meals for the 25 or so of us on the camp. He singlehandedly prepared three meals a day for everyone, in addition to ordering and managing the kitchen inventory. I offered my culinary services to ease his workload. Brad was a young Army specialist from Texas on his first combat deployment. He seemed like a nice kid and similarly introverted, so I never minded helping him out however I could. I'd always enjoyed cooking and baking for people and being in the kitchen was a welcome respite.

Over the course of a few weeks, I began to sense that Brad's attachment to me was growing romantically, but I shrugged it off and continued to offer him assistance in the kitchen. Everyone on the camp was on a first name basis with each other regardless of rank, which was common and expected in the special operations community. What was meant to help bolster trust and a sense of family served also to blur the lines of professionalism and military courtesies. I gave Brad the benefit of the doubt and assumed he remembered that I was still a captain in the Army at the end of the day, and therefore not interested in establishing a relationship that involved more than being professional acquaintances.

As April drew to a close, the already frayed relationships between Haley and myself and the ODA reached their breaking point in a cascade of unfortunate events. It played out like bad, scripted reality TV. I had long sensed Haley's allegiance was no longer to me or to the CST mission. She all but avoided me and spent hours each evening locked away in the aid station with Kyle under the pretense of giving English lessons to Farheed, which many on the camp had speculated wasn't actually what was going on in there. The unprofessional appearance the situation projected wasn't doing us any favors. But, I was too afraid of stirring up any more bad blood to confront Haley about her behavior, so I chose to turn a blind eye.

One evening after dinner I found myself in our community rec room, where a phone and a few computers with Internet allowed us to communicate with our families back home. I had been meaning to email my parents with an update, so I sat down on one of the couches nearby to wait for a computer to open up. My goal was to call or email my family once every week or so. I knew they worried a lot about me, so I did my best to allay their fears about my safety. Just as I had sat down at a computer to open my email, Darren, the Army satellite mechanic, came in and told me that Aaron and Haley were looking for me and needed to talk to me immediately. I sighed and closed the browser and made my way back to the operations center to look for Haley. It was dark, so I carefully made my way up the narrow stairs towards the hub of the camp, making sure to duck far enough under the stone archway. During our first week there I learned the hard way not to misjudge the height of the low opening. The archways caught many an unsuspecting forehead in the hours of darkness.

I wasn't exactly sure why Aaron and Haley were looking for me, or why they had sent Darren to find me, but a strange foreboding feeling told me that it wasn't good. I pushed open the door of the operations center to find Aaron alone at his desk, looking especially grim. He shoved away from his computer and gestured at me to sit.

"I'm only going to ask you this one time. Are you sleeping with Jake?" he fired at me, with crossed arms. He was wearing his usual pink Crocs, but they didn't seem as amusing as usual in contrast to the unexpected anger I could feel rising off him.

What? That was a serious question?

"No! What's going on?" I asked.

Aaron was mad. I could see his usually pale face turn bright pink to match his Crocs. His jaw was clenched.

"I heard a rumor. Is it or is it not true?" Aaron demanded.

I was utterly confused. I started wracking my brain to figure out where his accusation was coming from. I was blindsided

"No, who told you that?" I asked.

"Haley said she couldn't find you earlier tonight when she was looking for you, and that she has reason to believe you're sleeping with Jake. Brad apparently told her we could probably find you in Jakes room," he sighed.

I suspected Brad had strong feelings for me, but I didn't think his jealousy for my attention went so far as to accuse me of sleeping with someone on the camp. And then there was Haley. It appeared she had run with his offhanded comment and gone to Aaron before bothering to find out the truth from me. Her betrayal stung and I wracked my brain for her possible motive.

It was true that Jake and I had become friends since my arrival. He was easygoing and fun to be around, and treated me as an equal, while most other people on camp barely gave me the time of day. We frequently hung out around the fire pit in the evenings, but in full view of the operations center and always with other people. Was that enough to spark speculation? *Had* I been acting inappropriately and just didn't see it? I replayed every interaction that could have led an observer to think I had acted unprofessionally towards Jake. He was enlisted, and I clearly understood the boundaries of fraternization as an officer. Was it because he helped Haley and I build shelves for our room a few weeks ago? Was it because of that one time we worked out together in the gym by ourselves? Was I too friendly? Did I laugh too much around him? I didn't know the answers to any of my questions.

Aaron and I exchanged a few more tense words, and he reiterated the military's fraternization policy. I couldn't tell if he believed me when I said I wasn't sleeping with Jake. He was obviously perturbed by the unfolding drama and clearly wanted none of it on his camp. No one could blame him – he didn't ask for this. Whatever thin ice Haley and I had been walking on since our arrival had finally broken beneath our feet. I left the operations center as quickly as I could so he wouldn't see the tears that were fast approaching.

My mind raced as I stepped into our empty room and curled up in my bed, tears soaking my pillow. Vivid flashbacks to 2009 filled my head, when I had been wrongfully accused of being involved with Andy and attacked for my leadership. I remembered standing in a circle out by the back fence on KAF in the first gentle light of dawn. I was 23 again, dressed in a PT uniform, my M4 rifle slung across my chest. I watched as leaders in our unit took turns, one by one, openly accusing me of terrible things. I remembered how badly those arrows stung, and how impossibly alone I felt. Nothing I said or did then could clean up the shattered pieces of my reputation.

As my mind returned to my present circumstances overwhelming feelings of helplessness flooded me. I braced myself for the shockwave of vitriol that was sure to come from the rest of the people on the camp. At that moment, Haley opened the door and entered our room, carrying a handful of papers from her English lessons with Farheed.

"Hey! Are you okay?" she asked, seeing my tear streaked face.

"Haley, Aaron thinks I'm sleeping with Jake," I replied

morosely.

"Oh no, really? Why?" she asked with a tone of concern, which seemed a little too upbeat considering the circumstances. She was playing dumb, evidently.

"Maybe because you told him that!" I shot back defensively.

"Well, I did look for you and couldn't find you for like 10 minutes tonight when I looked for you. And Brad said you were probably sleeping together...perception is reality," she trailed off, shrugging.

"Because Brad is basically in love with me! It was jealous sarcasm, Haley!" I exclaimed.

In my absolute frustration I told her that this deployment was playing out exactly like my first one, where one small accusation turned into a tidal wave of venom against me. This was now the fifth time someone had accused me of fraternization in my career. I couldn't so much as be seen alone with a man in the military without it turning into fodder for gossip. Like the other times, there would be an inquiry or an investigation, and I would become a marked woman, subject to constant scrutiny.

Haley continued to play dumb the rest of the evening, refusing to see the disastrous implications of her accusations. She assumed a false air of empathy for my situation, but for the first time I could see right into the hollowness of it. I didn't sleep that night. Fear of what was to come had taken hold of me and there was no peace in my heart.

The next morning dawned overcast, as if the weather knew how I was feeling. I grabbed a quick breakfast from the kitchen and then went to find Jake. He and the team were getting ready for a mission, which Haley and I weren't permitted on, again. They were planning to cross the mountain range by helicopter and root out a small band of insurgents on the backside of the range. CST soldiers weren't allowed on any offensive missions, per protocol, so there was zero chance of us talking our way onto the flight. Aaron had made that clear. After Ashley White was killed, military leaders imposed severe restrictions on women in combat situations, especially CSTs. We were under a microscope at every moment. I pulled Jake aside from the group. I didn't care who saw us talking together – let them gossip and speculate. I wanted to get to the bottom of what was going on.

"Hey, dude, did Aaron call you in last night and ask you if we're sleeping together?" I asked.

"Um, nope, definitely not!" he replied with surprise in his voice.

Although unfair, it made sense to me. Even if the accusations were true it would be my fault, not his. And if they were unsubstantiated, I would still be exiled. I had seen the unfortunate pattern time and time again in the military, and I figured this time around would be no different. The accused woman was vilified and the man was generally left unscathed. I relayed the previous night's unfortunate events to Jake, my heart still sick at the thought of the accusations. He found it all to be strange, but wasn't surprised by it. He said he had known for a while that Haley wasn't looking out for anyone but herself. He suspected her actions were meant to distract us from her own inappropriate behavior and encouraged me to come forward to Aaron with what I knew about Haley's involvement with Kyle. Of course, it was all filled with speculation and hearsay, and I didn't want to muddy the waters any further. More than anything I wanted to keep the peace on our small camp and prayed everything would be resolved quickly.

I ran and grabbed my camera while the guys continued to prep their gear and weapons for the mission. It would be their first truly kinetic operation if everything played out the way they hoped it would. They were anxious to fire their weapons after weeks on end drinking tea and engaging in local diplomacy. Hank, the attack-trained German Shepherd, seemed to vocalize the tension in the air. He snarled and lunged against his lead at anyone who crossed in front of him too closely or lingered in an open doorway. He was more than ready to get to work. As I checked my zoom lens I saw that the team was taking the generator mechanic on the mission with them. I was positive that I had more weapons and tactical training than he did and silently sighed and rolled my eyes at the ridiculousness of it.

I planned to follow the crew out to the landing pad to get photos of them getting on the helicopter. Jake, who was responsible for communicating with aircraft in our area, always let me throw the purple and yellow smoke grenades to mark the helicopter landing zone, and I wasn't about to give up that small bit of fun to stay behind and pout that

I couldn't come along. Even if Haley and I had been allowed to come, there was no room in the helicopters for either of us. Aaron wanted his full team with him, plus his intel guys, canine team, and interpreters. The guys finished strapping on their kits and climbed onto the ATVs to make their way out to the landing pad. The two Blackhawk helos were due to arrive in less than 10 minutes. I began to snap pictures of Hank and his handler Ben on their way out, when I saw Haley out of the corner of my eye in full gear walking past me to the landing pad.

"Haley! What are you *doing*? We aren't allowed on this mission!" I said, a little too loudly.

"They changed their minds. They decided they really need me," she retorted, her voice dripping with condescension.

"What? Haley...!" I gasped. This was *not* supposed to happen.

She kept walking. I swallowed against the acrid resentment rising in the back of my throat as I watched her walk towards the incoming Blackhawks with the rest of the team. Without so much as a word to me she had gone over my authority to barter for a slot on the aircraft. Somehow, despite the events of the last 24 hours, I still expected her to be a team player and discuss going on the mission with me. I was ultimately responsible for her, for our team. We agreed to make all our operational decisions together. I felt betrayed and completely foolish for the blind trust I continued to have in her. Before I had too much time to feel sorry for myself, the helicopter roared overhead, the rotors sending a choking cloud of dust and rocks right into our faces. The team loaded up and quickly took off, smothering the landing zone with another wash of whirling dirt. After the dust cleared I watched the helicopters until they passed over the mountains before heading back into the quiet camp.

Brad, Megan, Darren and a few interpreters were the only other people left on the camp and I was in no mood to talk to any of them. Fatima had left a few days earlier to take leave and see her family back in the States. She was probably the only person I would have wanted to talk to there. I had deliberately left her out of the ongoing interpersonal struggles between Haley and I and was glad she wasn't present to witness the currently unfolding saga. I debated calling my parents while everyone was away on the mission, but decided not to. The situation hadn't quite reached a critical point that would prompt me to share it with my family or friends at home, and I really didn't want them to have another reason to worry about me.

I knew Brad would be in the kitchen preparing lunch for when the team returned, but I was emotionally exhausted and had no desire to confront his incendiary comments to Haley the night prior. Megan was in our room, having little work to do with the team out on mission, and next to Brad, she was the last person I wanted to strike up conversation with. We had hardly spoken more than a few sentences to each other since Haley and I arrived. Despite my attempt at friendliness she still hadn't warmed up to me.

After sulking around for a while I decided to pass the time by reading on the wooden bench next to the fire pit. The sun had broken through the clouds and the day was mild and pleasant. Life didn't seem so terrible in the stillness of the afternoon with no one around. An hour or so passed before Darren found me to let me know the team had radioed him – they were on their way back. We drove out to the landing pad on the ATVs and threw out colored smoke grenades to guide the incoming Blackhawks. The rotor wash kicked up a massive cloud of dust as they landed. I tried to snap a few photos of the team exiting the helicopters, before seeing they had a blindfolded detainee with them. I put down my camera out of respect for the sensitivity of the situation and immediately heard Haley screaming expletives at me to stop taking pictures. I sighed and did my best to conceal whatever indignant feelings I'm sure had immediately flashed across my face. Everyone loaded up onto the ATVs and we made our way back into the camp. The men released the detainee into the control of the Afghan Local Police and the rest of the team went to debrief in the operations center.

There was nothing in me that wanted to ask Haley about the mission, but I swallowed what little was left of my pride and willed myself to continue showing her kindness, at least outwardly. I followed her into our room and sat on my tough box while she took off her kit and put her gear away, intent on finding out how everything went. Unprompted, she launched immediately into a heroic retelling of how she stopped a potentially deadly situation in its tracks. The details were murky as to how she had been so critical to the situation, but I listened politely and said very little in return. She vocalized that the team would probably bring her along on missions from there on out rather than me, due to her finesse in handling the tense situation. Her words reeked of self-aggrandizing and made me seethe inwardly. I wished to be anywhere but there listening to Haley talk, yet I was too afraid to confront her latest charades and put an end to the burgeoning nonsense of the last two days.

Our room shared a thin wall with the operations center, and we could hear the team sergeant, Dan, addressing his men who were still gathered for their debriefing. With horror I listened as he rehashed the rumors about Jake and I, and ordered his team to speak to Haley and I as absolutely little as possible.

"If they're in here working and they're in your way, you tell them to get out. This is your ops center and you tell them what to do," he said. "Don't talk to them or have contact with them unless it's mission critical. Got it?"

There were a few murmurs of assent and some inquiries from the team about what had happened the night before. They were mostly in the dark, but had heard rumblings that something significant had happened. I felt instantly sick to my stomach and couldn't listen anymore. I knew this was just the beginning of more ugliness to come. I felt the all too familiar wave of helplessness pass over me. I was totally at the mercy of their perception. Reality no longer mattered, I could sense. Haley, however was completely unmoved by their discussion. She still blamed me for the trouble she had stirred up and maintained her innocence in the whole matter.

Over the next several days, things on the camp quickly got worse. Megan was moved to a different base to work, not before yelling at me and calling me a whore in front of several people on the camp. That was the most she had said to me since our arrival. She held me directly responsible for her removal. The men were hardly speaking to us, and every interaction with Haley brought bile into my mouth. She was arrogant and condescending, trying rather obviously to maintain superiority over me. I did my best to keep up appearances by making her a birthday cake and organizing a small party for her with the interpreters and a couple of the enablers that were still relatively unaware of what had gone on. I thought that if I continued to martyr myself in the name of peace that somehow the giant breach between us would heal. It was a faulty, hollow assumption that continued to feed into Haley's superiority complex and my growing self-pity. Fortunately, Jake was scheduled to return home shortly, having completed his six-month deployment, and I hoped his absence would further help deescalate the tension on the camp. If he was gone, no one could gossip about us anymore, I hoped.

A few days later Haley and I were awakened early one morning to Dan pounding on our door. I crawled out of bed and opened the door, squinting sleepily against the bright daylight.

"Ya'll are moving. Pack up your stuff and have it out by this afternoon," he barked.

He explained that his team didn't have enough space in their rooms and they were claiming our room for themselves. Within a matter of a few hours Haley and I found ourselves hauling our gear to the transient quarters at the back corner of camp, which were reserved generally for visitors and guests. The room was fairly small, but with Megan gone and Fatima on leave, there was enough room for us. I claimed a bunk after we finished moving everything out of our old room and began to unpack my sheets and blankets. The plywood bunk frame was too small for the mattress, which curled up on both ends. But, it was a place to lay my head, and I was drained from lack of sleep and the emotional events of the previous days. Half-awake nightmares had plagued me for the last several nights and prevented me from having any truly restful sleep. The images that flashed through my dreams were shadowy red and black figures. Fear and anxiety had become visible shapes in my subconscious. There was a gripping darkness to them, and they kept me in a fitful twilight between awake and asleep. I put my headphones on and laid down for a nap, praying for a sliver of peace to find my heart.

I woke up an hour or two later to find Haley was gone. It was nearly dinnertime. I stood up and stretched and saw out of the corner of my eye a folder sitting on Haley's bed with white paper forms sticking out. Without much closer inspection I could tell exactly what the forms were: DA Form 2823s, otherwise known as the standard Army Sworn Statement forms. They were legal documents, written under oath and signed by witnesses. The Army used them to gather information for investigations. My curiosity got the best of me, and I picked them up to see what was written on them. I was a quick reader and confident I could scan over the documents before Haley returned.

Three stapled together pages were filled with carefully typed allegation after allegation of my unbecoming conduct during my month and a half on the camp. Haley's name and social security number on the top of the page gave little doubt as to the source of the document. Aaron and Dan's signature under the witness blocks meant that they had read the statement, too. Hurt and anger welled up in my chest as I read the accusations. Meredith was consistently unprofessional. Meredith had thrown medical supplies around the aid station in a fit of rage during IV training. Meredith had treated Kyle disrespectfully during one of his instructional classes by looking at her watch too often. Meredith didn't support the ODA's mission. Meredith was mentally unstable and I (Haley) am very concerned for her wellbeing. Meredith had back pain because she couldn't handle stress and had to be babied at all times. Meredith might be sleeping around, because people couldn't locate her for ten whole minutes one night. Meredith didn't truly understand the CST mission. Meredith was a weak leader, unprofessional, unlikeable and unqualified. She had filled three pages with her own twisted perceptions of me.

I had become so insecure over the last several weeks that I wondered if maybe she was correct about some of her accusations. She had me so convinced of my own shortcomings that maybe I actually *was* a failure. I couldn't see that she had been gaslighting me all along. Shoving the papers back underneath her folder, my heart pounded and the sudden taste of metal was on my tongue. Still, I couldn't bring myself to confront her.

After another restless night, the day dawned warm and clear. Jake was scheduled to fly out and return home that day, to my relief. The rest of us on camp were recruited by Dan to help clean and de-clutter all the common areas and kitchen. Boxes upon boxes of candy and toiletries from well-meaning organizations needed to be sorted through, and a winter's worth of mud swept away. I was grateful for the distraction and an excuse to not have to talk to anyone. The cleanup effort was well underway when Aaron gathered everyone on the camp outside the ops center, including the interpreters. He announced a surprise inspection and told us that no one was allowed to leave the immediate area while Dan checked every person's room and personal belongings for contraband. Apparently, Kyle and Ryan had conducted an inventory of the aid station supplies the day prior and found several controlled narcotics were missing from their locked safe. The aid station was kept locked whenever the medics weren't actively working inside, so whoever had taken the drugs had made a significant effort to steal the keys and enter when no one was around.

While Dan conducted his searches with the medics, Aaron asked each of us if we knew anything about the missing medication. No one came forward with information. Each of us were as shocked as the next person. We stood around in silence for several tense moments wondering what was happening. It didn't take long for Dan to return to the group. He announced that he had found a stash of contraband medication and hashish hidden underneath one of the refrigerators in the kitchen. Khan, the local man we paid to help out around camp, came forward and told Dan and Aaron that Brad had been paying him to buy hashish and drugs off the local economy and deliver them in private. After a brief interrogation, Brad also admitted that he had been breaking into the aid station to steal the controlled medication. I couldn't believe what was happening, or that so many things were falling apart so quickly on the camp.

We finished our duties in silence as Brad was taken into makeshift custody. His cot was moved into the ops center where someone was assigned to watch him at all times. Aaron notified the AOB (Advanced Operating Base) to inform them of the situation. The AOB was our next higher headquarters, run by Navy SEALs. They oversaw all the special operations in Zabul province and the ODA reported to them. The AOB agreed to send a helicopter and military police to escort Brad to Bagram for immediate drug testing. I could see in Aaron's face that he wanted to make the previous two weeks of his life disappear. The events on his camp didn't reflect well on him or his team. He bore the brunt of responsibility for the good and the bad that happened under his watch. No one envied his position. Later that afternoon, as the shock of the new events began to wear off, Haley confronted me.

"I want you to know that I called the AOB commander and he wants to pull us out of this site. There will be an investigation because of everything that you've done. Dan and Aaron agreed that it's best given what's happened," Haley explained, her voice heavy with superiority.

"So you've been going to the team behind my back," I concluded. "Why didn't you tell me you talked to the AOB?"

"Well, the plan is for you to get sent home so I can come back here and finish the deployment by myself," she said.

I was floored.

"For *real*? You've actually been working this behind my back with the team just so you can see me get sent home," I retorted.

"It's for the best," she replied. "They need me here."

This conversation needed to end. The smugness mixed with counterfeit innocence in her voice sent me into an internal rage. I was irate and completely flabbergasted. I had volunteered to deploy and put myself on the line, to do an important job that I really believed in. Months of training had prepared me for this, and here we were wasting our time with her juvenile ploys. The entire situation seemed incredibly unfair, and I couldn't understand why it was happening to me.

I went to the back hallway in the operations center and called my parents in relative privacy. It was time they knew everything that had happened. I sobbed into the phone, relaying the previous days' events. My mom, ever the calm one in a crisis, prayed for me over the phone as I sniffed and wiped away the tears that were still falling. She encouraged me to remember that God would take care of me. Even if everything fell apart, He had the final word, and my integrity and the truth would win out in the end.

"Honey, this is only one rung in the ladder of your career. You will be ok no matter what happens," she assured me.

I wanted to believe that's what would happen, but I had seen injustice doled out too many times in the Army to really put my full faith in God in that moment. My entire world existed inside those mud walls and it was falling apart quickly.

The next couple days passed in a blur. Brad was escorted away and Aaron soon received word that he had tested positive for six illicit drugs during his urinalysis. Haley and I packed all our belongings in preparation to leave for good. We hadn't even been in Shajoy for two months and were already on our way out. It felt like the end of the road. Aaron let us know that a ground convoy from the AOB was scheduled to drop some supplies off and take Haley and I away to their base a couple hours away. We didn't know what was going to happen there, if we would stay long, or any details of the days to come. I assumed there would be an investigation of sorts and Haley and I would be moved to another location for the rest of the deployment. The likelihood of getting assigned a new partner was incredibly slim, so I made up my mind to pull out every last stop to mend the fracture in our partnership. Nine months was a long time to be totally miserable and I still believed we could reconcile our issues.

Chapter 15

The Prizefighter

Mid-afternoon in early May, Haley and I were standing outside the camp entrance with our belongings packed into a large box for transport, dressed in full kit and protective gear for the trip to the AOB. The small convoy arrived, kicking up clouds of powdery dust, and before too long I was sitting in the back of an armored truck, bumping over rough dirt roads through the village. After about an hour we arrived at the AOB, a small compound within FOB Lagman, a large U.S. and Romanian-run base, as the sun was starting to set. I had been to Lagman numerous times during my previous tour and it felt strange to be there again under such different circumstances.

After dismounting from the vehicle, I stood in the gravel lot while a forklift downloaded our box of gear and watched resignedly as Haley quickly made her way over to the convoy commander, an infantry staff sergeant who worked for the AOB. From a distance I watched her brief him, both of them occasionally looking my way. I could only imagine what terrible things she was telling him about me. She had a gift for manipulation and knew how to get people on her side. She had poisoned my mind for weeks, making me think something was wrong with me, and I still couldn't shake it from my system. I wanted to rise up and defend myself, but a voice inside me wondered if I had brought all of this trouble on myself. I felt like a prisoner in custody, totally at the mercy of people who didn't know me, but knew everything about me. I may as well have had a scarlet letter on my chest.

That evening Haley and I were settled into our new temporary accommodations, 20-foot shipping containers, which had been modified into housing units, with locking doors and a bed. I breathed a huge sigh of relief to find we each would have our own room for however long we would stay there. The privacy and silence was going to be bliss. There were hot showers, running water and flushing toilets. It was a respectable consolation prize for getting moved from the VSP where we had to burn our own waste and wash our hands with bottled water. After settling in, I found the small dining facility nearby and went to grab dinner. I was surprised to see Haley was already in there eating, with what appeared to be her new friends, a small group of SEALs and Army soldiers. I couldn't bring myself to sit with her or even look her way. I took my paper tray of food back to my room to eat alone, shoving open the screen door of the dining facility with my foot as I left and letting it slam behind me. There wasn't a chance that anyone was on my side after talking with Haley, who seemed to be happily spreading tales of my "offenses" to whoever would listen.

After dinner Haley came and knocked on my door. We hadn't had a real conversation in a few days, so we were due for another painful confrontation. I warily let her in and closed the door behind her, uneager to hear what gem of misinformation she was going to drop on me next. She told me she was getting moved to Bagram. Somehow a malaria pill had gotten lodged in her esophagus and she needed to get it checked out at an advanced medical facility. She would be leaving the next day on a flight, and I would stay put and wait for further instructions from the AOB. Haley was confident that when it was all said and done, I would be sent home disgraced and she would return to the VSP in Shajoy. She informed me that she had already relayed our circumstances to our CST manager and would see her in Bagram shortly to confirm her plans. Hot tears of anger and hurt welled up in my eyes, and threatened to spill over. I really didn't want to cry in front of Haley, but I couldn't stop the flood.

"Why are you doing all this, Haley? I don't understand. This storm you created could end my career." I pleaded with her, desperately trying to strike some chord of empathy. The more I saw how cold and callous she was, the harder I tried to make her understand the destructive magnitude of what she had set into motion. She was unflinching. Even if I had come to her with a severed limb I doubt she would have done much more than raise an eyebrow at me. Then, with the well-timed precision of a boxer, Haley delivered the knockout blow.

"Mer, I think this is God's way of telling you that you're on the wrong path. Maybe this just isn't for you," Haley cooed in her sweetly condescending voice. "Besides, there's no way *anyone* is going to let you operate in country after all of this."

"Maybe so," I resigned, devastated. Haley left my room in triumph. A fresh wave of tears erupted out of me as I closed the door behind her. I was overcome by the helplessness, anger, and utter confusion. I couldn't make sense of anything that was happening to me. I felt like a total failure. If God had called me here, then why *was* He letting everything fall apart? It felt like He had broken a promise to me. This was supposed to be it, *my* big game, *my* big chance to do something epic and purposeful, and here I was about to get thrown out of the game. I was so lost in my own circumstances that I couldn't see that God still had a purpose for me, just like he spoke into me the first night in Shajoy. Even in the midst of the struggle, He was still there making a way for me. The misguided actions of other people didn't change that.

Haley left for Bagram the next day, leaving me in relative peace before I was set to relocate to the Special Operations Task Force East (SOTF-E) headquarters in Uruzgan Province. Almost immediately the toxic cloud that had been hovering over my head for weeks began to evaporate, and I felt light and free. The future was still uncertain, but I was finally relieved of Haley's oppressive presence. I spent my first full day at the AOB indulging in rest, laying in my sleeping bag reading the *Twilight* series on my Kindle. I had no mission, no agenda, and it was just what my weary soul needed. After a luxurious post-lunch nap, I went out in search of the gym, ready to stretch my legs a bit after a day of leisure. The gym was considerably larger and better stocked than the goat-scented tent on the VSP. By most standards, it was still a poor excuse for a fitness center. The weights were mismatched and rusty, covered in a film of dust. I didn't care – it looked like heaven to me. Only one or two other people were in the gym at the time, including the young staff sergeant who had led the convoy from Shajoy to the AOB. I knew being a female in special ops territory meant I was a bit of a spectacle, so I was grateful there weren't more people there to gawk and stare at me. I popped my headphones in and started my workout playlist on my iPod, the universal signal for "don't talk to me while I'm working out." I lifted weights until I felt sufficiently exhausted and collapsed into a sweaty pile on an empty section of floor to stretch out. I saw the staff sergeant walk towards me, looking like he wanted to say something. Warily, I pulled my headphones out and braced myself for his criticism.

"Hey, ma'am. I couldn't help but notice your workout," he said tentatively. "That was the most intelligently planned workout I've ever seen in this gym."

I prided myself on my workout programming. I was a woman with a plan and knew how to put together an effective lifting session.

"Um, thanks," I replied skeptically. *What does this guy want?*

He continued, "I really just have the feeling that you aren't who everyone says you are. I've heard you're a dumb sorority chick who's been partying it up and causing trouble, but that doesn't match up with who I'm seeing in here. I know it's weird, I just feel like I can't believe the rumors."

I was too stunned to reply in the moment. This man was living proof that not *everyone* was against me. He was the fresh voice of reason in a whirlwind of speculation and finger pointing. He introduced himself as Staff Sgt. Talavares and we chatted for a few minutes about weightlifting, and then walked toward the chow hall to grab a post-workout snack. I was worried someone from the AOB would see me with a male soldier and start a new wave of unfounded rumors. Fortunately, the chow hall was empty as we grabbed protein shakes and sat down to continue our conversation. I didn't want to talk about Haley or what I had been through and felt eager to down my entire shake and leave. Nervously I looked over my shoulder as if being in the full view of the public with a male soldier was a crime I'd be caught and punished for. Sgt. Talavares could sense my skittishness and offered some simple encouragement before we parted ways.

He asked bluntly, "If a 10 year old tells you you're stupid and ugly, are you going to believe him? No. So why would you believe these people when they tell you you're a failure?"

I chuckled, appreciating his blunt perspective, and returned to my bunk to shower and get ready for dinner. I never saw Sgt. Talavares again, but his simple kindness in the gym that day made an overwhelming impression on me.

The next few days of my purgatory passed much the same as

the first day. There was little to do on the compound besides workout, sleep, eat and check email on the rec room computers. Much to my relief, nightmares no longer held my sleep captive, and my clarity of mind was rapidly returning. I periodically sent Facebook messages to Haley to check on her, and received replies that she would be in Bagram longer than originally planned, along with a chastisement for posting a deployment picture on my personal page, which she deemed inappropriate. Secretly her absence was a relief. There were still at least a few more days without her before being reunited, and I was unable to exert any sympathy for her health aside from routine inquiries.

I also spoke with our head CST manager in Bagram, an Army Captain named Maria, who could offer me no more information about our future other than there would be an investigation. She was confident everything would blow over, but I didn't share her optimism. Haley and I would meet up in Uruzgan Province at the SOTF-E to await additional instructions. Flights to the headquarters from the busy base left fairly regularly, so I was able to reserve a seat on the outgoing aircraft on the fourth day after our arrival.

Chapter 16

An Oasis

The morning of my departure dawned clear and bright. The AOB was at a full 2,000 feet elevation lower than Shajoy, and the temperature was much warmer than I was used to, even in mid-May. I arrived at the small passenger terminal building at the designated time to check in and make sure there was room on the flight for my large box of gear. The only other people waiting for the flight to Uruzgan were a few civilian contractors and an interpreter or two. After everyone checked in we moved outside to a holding area near the flight line to await the incoming aircraft. It was now midday, and the heat was making the horizon shimmer and wave. There was no overhead cover, and the concrete barrier walls kept any breeze from reaching us.

After searing uncomfortably in the heat for almost an hour, we finally saw a C-130 taxi toward us and come to a stop nearby. The air crew dropped the tail ramp and we scurried towards the gaping mouth of the airplane. As my eyes adjusted to the dark interior I saw that the inside of the plane had been stripped. There were no seats in sight, save one front-facing Captain's style chair towards the front. The flight chief offered me the seat, being the only other uniformed person on board. As I buckled in I watched in mild horror as the crew sat the rest of the passengers down on the deck of the aircraft and secured them to the floor with a nylon ratchet strap. It was spartan military ingenuity at its finest – unorthodox but relatively safe.

It was oppressively hot in the belly of the plane. There was no air circulation and save for the cockpit, the plane had no climate control mechanisms. I hoped when we got up in the air it would cool off some. Otherwise it was going to be a miserable flight. The passengers were all wearing body armor and helmets, adding to the discomfort. Finally, we began to taxi, and with a loud rattle the plane rocketed upward. Combat takeoffs and landings were always a little harrowing, and I was grateful to be buckled into an actual seat. I closed my eyes and waited for the plane to level out. It was supposed to be a short hop over a mountain range to get to the SOTF-E headquarters. Twenty minutes and we would be back on the ground. Without warning the plane plunged down out of the sky and banked hard to the right. The steep snowcapped mountains outside the small window disappeared and I saw nothing but blue sky. Suddenly the plane shot back up into the air, banking hard again in the opposite direction. I breathed in deeply through my nose and gripped the seat arms.

The Taliban didn't have aircraft and most of their artillery was ancient at best, so the odds that the pilot was trying to outmaneuver enemy fire over the remote mountains was slim. More than likely, he was either showing off or trying to terrify the small group of civilians strapped to the floor of his aircraft. I guessed the latter. I removed my helmet and rolled up my sleeves in an attempt to try to cool my overheated body as the pilot continued his rollercoaster maneuvers, which continued for the duration of the flight. At regular intervals over the sound of the rotors I could hear the other passengers gasping as the plane violently dropped and shot up again into the air, following the steep contours of the mountain range between Zabul and Uruzgan Provinces. My queasy stomach reeled and I willed myself to not throw up. I had already sweated through my uniform.

After what seemed like an eternity, the plane finally took its final plunge, landing roughly on the small airstrip inside the U.S. base and rumbling to a gradual stop. As I peeled my sweaty and shaky legs from the chair and turned around I saw that more than one of the passengers strapped to the floor had gotten sick on themselves. I was still on the verge of getting sick myself, and I couldn't get off the plane fast enough. The heat, the smell, the mess. A smiling pilot and his flight crew emerged from the cockpit and unstrapped the passengers from the floor. We all but sprinted off the tail ramp into the blinding sunlight, grateful to be on steady ground. A representative from the task force was waiting outside with a vehicle to drive myself and a female interpreter, who also survived the flight from hell, to their compound.

"I got sick. Twice!" she said, looking a little green as we loaded into the SUV. "That was the worst flight I've ever been on!"

I nodded my head slightly in assent, afraid that if I moved too much I might get sick, too. I was still reeling. The soldier drove us across the camp to the first tent in a line of large identical tents, where I would be staying until further notice. A wooden "Female" sign adorned the top of the door. He pointed out the bathrooms, dining facility, laundry and TOC buildings before leaving us to settle in. I chose an unoccupied cot in the dim tent and dropped my assault pack on top of it. I looked around at the other cots and breathed a sigh of relief when I didn't see any of Haley's stuff anywhere. A few other women were sleeping or listening to music with headphones on their bunks. Haley would be there soon enough, but for now I had a little peace, and much welcome air conditioning.

After lying perfectly still for several minutes on my cot, I decided I was no longer at great risk of tossing my lunch and warily made my way up to the TOC. Protocol required me to report my presence to Capt. Johnson and see what information he could offer me about what was to happen next. We had only spoken a few times via email, so I wasn't sure what to expect from him. The TOC was crowded and busy, but I was able to track down Capt. Johnson after a few inquiries. He looked tired and overworked, and I was one more problem for him to handle. His office was a table and computer in the middle of the bustling main room with little privacy to talk about sensitive matters. He suggested we walk over to the dining facility, which was empty mid-afternoon.

We sat down on a bench at a sticky vinyl-topped table inside. Industrial fans on the walls moved a breeze through the warm cafeteria. Small flat screens on the walls played an NBA championship game. People in the stands were drinking cold Pepsi and eating popcorn, the humanness of which seemed strangely comforting to me. I absently wondered who was watching the game back in the States. It fascinated me how life went on uninterrupted. It all seemed light-years away from a desolate combat zone. Capt. Johnson brought me back to the present. He turned to me with his elbows on the table, his fingers interlocked, like a businessman about to have a serious talk with a client. His neatly trimmed mustache seemed out of place on his thin face and did little to hide his youth. He seemed uncomfortable with whatever he was about to say.

"The first thing we need to do here is make sure you're okay," he said straightforwardly. "There are some concerns brought forward that you may be wanting to hurt yourself and we really just want to make sure you're alright."

I wondered who "we" were. I knew that he and the task force commander, at the very least, had seen Haley's sworn statement, in which she had closed with a paragraph stating she thought I might hurt myself. She had written it like a concerned friend, but it was just another act in her dramatic performance.

I sighed heavily and explained that there wasn't any foundation to his concerns. I was miserable and stressed, yes, but not in danger of becoming completely unhinged. As I spoke a few tears slipped embarrassingly out of my eyes, despite my determination to be as unemotional as possible. Capt. Johnson looked down at his clasped hands, unsure of what to do about a crying woman in his presence. He finally prompted me to give my side of the story, starting from when Haley and I arrived in Shajoy. I briefly rehashed the events of the last month and a half as objectively as possible. As I spoke I realized how truly absurd the whole story sounded. It all seemed petty and childish in retrospect. I wanted nothing more than for it to be behind me so I could get back to work. He listened without saying much until I finished.

"The commander is probably going to do a basic inquiry to get more details about what happened so we can decide what to do with you and Haley," Capt. Johnson said. "We'll need your written sworn statement at some point."

I was looking forward to a chance to set the record straight. I didn't know if anyone would believe me over Haley, but I was eager to put the truth out there, ideally before she arrived from Bagram and started a new misinformation campaign. Capt. Johnson couldn't give me any idea when the inquiry would happen, or what would happen to Haley or me. The decisions were high above his level of authority and he was merely the messenger. I left him feeling only marginally better about my situation.

The next morning, I made my way back up to the TOC to check in with Capt. Johnson again and let him know I was still alive. The last thing he needed on his plate was to babysit a fellow captain, but I was required to report to him twice a day for accountability purposes regardless. He had no new information to give me, so I walked over to the chow hall to eat breakfast. A large array of fresh fruits, yogurt and standard American breakfast fare greeted me. It definitely beat the frozen French toast sticks and Clif Bars that I had been accustomed to over the last three months. I picked a seat by myself with my tray and silently willed the hordes of Navy SEALs and Green Berets filing in after their morning workouts to stay away. I wasn't in the mood for conversation or stares, so I finished my breakfast quickly and left.

Back in the tent, a young woman in a Navy uniform was settling in to one of the few remaining cots. I recognized her vaguely as one of the CST women on a team with my friend from the CST training course, Kate, an Army lieutenant. She and Amy had been part of many of the same weekly video conferences as Haley and I. She introduced herself as Allie. She was at the headquarters for a short time in order to refit with some of the other Navy CST women before heading back out to their remote operating site. Allie was kind and gentle, with an open and friendly demeanor. We bonded almost immediately and her extension of friendship refreshed me. Allie had heard through Kate that I was at SOTF-E, and knew bits and pieces of what had happened in Shajoy. I gave her the highlight reel of the last two months, working hard to keep the acrid bitterness out of my voice. She listened with calm empathy while I spoke, and then offered heartening encouragement to keep the faith. Allie drew on her deep faith in God to give me a small flicker of hope that things could and *would* get better in the days to come.

With nothing better to do than kill time, Allie and I decided to explore the base. She had been to the headquarters several times before and knew her way around fairly well. We walked towards the edge of the American base, where a dusty entry control point separated it from a conjoining Australian base, formerly operated by Dutch forces. On the other side of the base we perused small Afghan shops and ate at the large dining facility, which we were thrilled to find had an ice machine. Cold beverages were few and far between in country, and ice was an absolute rarity. The food was standard military fare, but we relished our cold Gatorades in the air conditioning before strolling back to our tent in the midday heat. Allie's friendship felt like an oasis in the searing desert. She not only helped to carry my emotional burdens, but gave me words of peace and hope in return.

The following day I decided to check out the gym situation at the camp. It had to be at least marginally better than the last two gyms. And I had nothing but time, it appeared. Whoever was in charge of my fate seemed in no particular hurry to send me on my way. I put on my longest pair of shorts and a tan uniform t-shirt, hoping to draw as little attention to myself as possible. Working out was one of the only things helping maintain somewhat of a routine while hopping from place to place. It was also my little piece of sanity in the absolute uncertainty of my future.

The gym was housed in a large building on the far side of the TOC, within walking distance of the sleep tent. I pulled open the door and stood briefly in shock as my eyes adjusted to my surroundings. A large glass-front cooler held bottles of water, right next to the check-in desk, topped with clean, folded towels. The gym was massive, rivaling the nicest military gym I'd ever been inside. Professional wooden lifting platforms, each adorned with a shellacked Navy SEAL emblem and outfitted with a squat and pull-up rack, anchored the center of the room. Large mirrors lined the walls, which held racks of kettlebells and dumbbells of every weight, each matched with its partner. A line of rowing machines, a climbing rope, treadmills, ellipticals, and a stretching area rounded out the impressive and well-stocked gym. I sighed and rolled my eyes to myself. SEALs were so spoiled.

But, my snobbery wasn't going to keep me from enjoying the beautiful fitness oasis I'd stumbled upon. Deep inside, I was incredibly grateful for a pristine, spacious gym to kill some time in, especially after making do in the other austere gyms. And, there was an adorable German Shepherd dog walking on a treadmill in the far corner, so who was I to be upset? So, the gym became my daily refuge. Working out anchored my mind, albeit temporarily, which threatened to unravel with anxiety and fear. Every afternoon in the heat of the day I would work out, lifting hard and heavy, until a flood of endorphins kicked in. I was getting stronger physically, but my mind was still subject to fits of panic.

Chapter 17

The Dog Days

Haley arrived in full force from Bagram that afternoon. Allie, who had begun packing up to leave for her operating site, whispered quietly to me that she had arrived while I was in the gym. Her face looked guilty and slightly panicked as she relayed the news. Indeed, Haley's familiar sleeping bag stretched out on a cot a few spaces over from mine. She wasn't in the tent, so I assumed she was at the TOC checking in with Capt. Johnson. Allie's impending departure made me sad and also grateful. I was glad she wasn't staying around to get tangled in our ugly mess. Her brief presence had renewed my faith and given me something that I hadn't felt in a long time – hope.

Allie and I said our goodbyes, and then I headed to the shower to clean up before dinner. When I returned, a hot pink envelope was laid neatly on my pillow. Perfect script on the front read: *To my Sister in Christ, with lots of love.* Allie had left a beautiful note of encouragement. With a full heart I opened up my worn copy of *My Utmost for His Highest* by Oswald Chambers, which had been neglected at the bottom of my tough box the last month. I needed to hear from God. I had become so tightly wound up in my own anxiety that I hadn't taken much time to actually talk to God, other than a few despairing, tearful prayers. Oswald himself may as well have written the day's reading just for me, it was almost laughably what I needed to hear.

"Either Jesus Christ is a deceiver, having deceived even Paul, or else some extraordinary thing happens to someone who holds on to the love of God when the odds are totally against him. Logic is silence in the face of each of these things which come against him. Only one thing can account for it – the love of God in Christ Jesus. *'Out of the wreck I rise', every time."*

I read the passage over and over, just to make sure there wasn't something I was missing, like a list of conditions for God's love. Surely, He wouldn't *always* have my back. Maybe I needed to learn a tough lesson about trusting people, or maybe my circumstances were deserved punishment for not being a model leader. But there it was, truth written in black and white. *"In all things we are more than conquerors[15]"* and *"who shall separate us from the love of Christ[16]?"* I felt a small, trembling thread of faith reach out and tether my heart to the promise that no human scheme could separate me from the immeasurable love of God. I finally began to understand that the odds would never be against me as long as God was for me – and He was *always* for me. I could step out into the unknown, even with all odds against me, and into victory.

Soon after Haley's arrival a room opened up for me inside the main female housing building. I was incredibly grateful to have a space myself and not have to awkwardly avoid Haley in the small tent we shared with several other women. The quarters were simple, but heavenly. The small room was air conditioned and had a real bed with a mattress in it, and an Ethernet cable for Internet. It may as well have been the Hilton. When I wasn't working out or eating, I napped in the quiet room or watched movies on my laptop. The solitude was healing.

After the fourth or fifth straight day of check-ins with Capt. Johnson (who never had any new information to report), I finally got word that something was happening. Now that Haley and I were both on the same base, the looming investigation would begin, and they needed my sworn statement. I sat at a computer in the TOC for an hour, furiously typing out a rebuttal to Haley's statement. Whether any of what I said would make a difference, I didn't know. After finishing, I printed off the statement, roping in two witnesses to sign it. Capt. Johnson administered my oath, and then completed the final signature on the last page of the document.

Minutes later, he introduced me to the Navy JAG officer who

---

[15] Romans 8:37, as quoted in *My Utmost for His Highest*

[16] Romans 8:35, as quoted in *My Utmost for His Highest*

was in charge of the inquiry. He led me into his small office, which I strongly suspected was designed as a closet rather than a workspace. He shuffled some papers around and pulled out a typed form, which outlined the two main allegations against me. *1. Fraternization 2. Conduct unbecoming an officer.* He asked me to read the charges and provide my signature, stating that I understood what Haley had brought against me. Then he presented a second document outlining my rights as a service member under investigation. I was allowed a lawyer, should I request it, and was not required to make a statement. There was a list of rights and stipulations to read through, and without hesitation waived my right to remain silent. I *wanted* to make a statement. I was ready.

The JAG officer, a benign-looking Navy lieutenant, offered me a seat and took out his notepad and pen. He explained that this wasn't a formal investigation, just a general inquiry for the commander to see if a formal investigation would be required. The lieutenant worked directly for the head of the task force, a battle-hardened Navy SEAL named Commander Harrison. He began his questioning.

"Did you ever throw medical supplies across the aid station while at the VSP?" he asked.

In that moment I became acutely aware that this was a colossal waste of his time. The special operations forces in the region were busy fighting actual battles and had real life or death matters to deal with. This inquiry was my whole world and occupied all free space in my mind, but it paled in comparison to the war happening outside. I suddenly felt self-conscious and childish.

"No, I did not," I answered. I remembered getting frustrated with several unsuccessful attempts at starting an IV during medical training with Kyle and Ryan, but I *definitely* hadn't thrown anything.

The questioning continued, addressing each of Haley's accusations of unprofessionalism against me. Somehow, I managed to not cry during the interview. My knees were shaky and I was nervous sweating, but my voice was steady. Then, his questions turned to my leadership competency. I did my best to explain the CST's operational hardships at the VSP. Shajoy District was non-permissive. Even the ODA struggled to make significant headway in their relationships with the villagers. It was the nature of the region. He asked about my

141

relationship with Haley, in depth, and I tried to be as honest as possible without sounding vindictive. I left out the parts about her inappropriate behavior. I was still clinging desperately to what I thought was the high ground, not wanting to draw more attention to the already murky situation. Next, he questioned me about my relationship with Jake, and what Brad's role was in the whole ordeal. My explanation sounded no less absurd than when I had recounted it to Capt. Johnson a week prior. The JAG exhausted his questions, and then put his pen and legal pad down on his cluttered desk.

"I'm not supposed to say this to you as a JAG, since this is an official inquiry. But this all seems like a bunch of gossipy, high school bulls***," he said with a sigh. "I can't see what you did wrong here, but it's up to the commander to make the final determination."

He assured me his full report and investigation would go to the commander's desk soon, and it wouldn't be long before I would know the outcome. I knew I wasn't out of the woods yet, but his words comforted me greatly. I emailed Jake after the interview. He was already back at home, enjoying the comforts of stateside living. My main questions was if SOTF-E had interviewed him or initiated an investigation. He had been there for several days waiting for a flight on his way home. He confirmed that no one had spoken to him or asked for a sworn statement about our rumored involvement with each other. I was the sole target of the witch hunt, it appeared.

The next several days passed much the same. I ate, checked in with Capt. Johnson, worked out in the magical gym, showered, ate, napped, ate, avoided Haley, and waited. Finally, on May 29, nearly a month after we'd left Shajoy, I got the word I'd been waiting for. Capt. Johnson called me into the TOC and said the charges against me had been cleared. The JAG had found no evidence of wrongdoing on my part. He believed my behavior was reasonably within what was expected from a junior captain, and cited Haley as the sole instigator of the issues in Shajoy. I felt vindicated, but still peeved that I'd been taken out of the fight for a full month. Soon, Haley and I would meet Cdr. Harrison and find out our new assignments.

In the meantime, I received a letter from my Grandma Dolly. She had carefully typed it with her old typewriter, signing her name in pen at the bottom. My parents had been keeping her updated on my situation. She was a fierce prayer warrior, and went to battle every day for those she loved.

Meredith, all of us who love you realize you are experiencing some of the toughest tests of your young life, and that the adversary is doing his best to poison your thoughts through the actions of others – and I want you to know that in the name of our Lord Jesus Christ, I stand with you in denouncing those evil thrusts. "Ye shall no need to fight in this battle; set yourself, stand ye still and see the salvation of the Lord with you." (2ⁿᵈ Chron 20:15b&17)

Her words filled me with comfort. *Thank you, Grandma.* I needed continual reminding that God was on my side, fighting the unseen battle.

Memorial Day came and went, and the first week of June was coming to a close. Time was moving at a snail's pace. Then at last, Cdr. Harrison asked to meet with Haley and I after his daily briefing. The next morning, Capt. Johnson stood with me outside the commander's briefing room in the TOC. He was present to mediate the interaction between Cdr. Harrison and Haley and I. The door swung open after several minutes and the commander's staff filed out. Haley was already sitting at the long table close to him. She had apparently sat in on the meeting to get a leg up on me with the boss. I sat down on the opposite side of the table with Capt. Johnson, waiting for the stragglers to clear the room. After several minutes, the commander addressed us.

"Lieutenant," he said looking at Haley, "There's a spot for you with the Navy CST." He named a nearby base. "You'll be released to the AOB. Captain Morris, there is no longer any room for you to operate within the region," he said without making eye contact. "I'm releasing you to your CST headquarters for reassignment." My heart sank. Haley was being sent back out into the field, and I would have to go to Bagram to see if there was any place for me to work. SOTF-E was essentially wiping their hands of me. Bagram was so far removed from what was happening with the units on the ground. I didn't want to go and endure another round of agonizing waiting and scrutiny. For not being in the wrong I sure felt like I was being punished.

"Yes, sir," I managed to croak out.

The commander dismissed us and we left in silence. I went back to my room and packed. There was a flight leaving to Bagram soon, and

I would be on it. I walked to the TOC one last time to check out with Capt. Johnson before my flight out. As I approached the building, Cdr. Harrison intercepted me, his dark sunglasses reflecting the morning sun. I tensed.

"Let me tell you something, Captain. Even though my JAG cleared you, I still have a gut feeling you did wrong. I think you did sleep with that guy, and you're a failure as a leader." He was too close to my face now. "Girls like you give the CST program a bad name. If it were up to me I'd scrap the whole thing. I don't want any of you in my task force." He walked away and I stood in stunned silence for a minute before continuing on my way. It was hard not to take his words personally. The CST women in Afghanistan were my friends and sisters. They were some of the most passionate, intelligent, hardworking women I'd ever had the privilege to meet, and I didn't take kindly to being told we didn't belong. My blood boiled all the way to my flight.

It was mid-afternoon when I reached the flight line. I dreaded the flight. Bagram was at least an hour away by aircraft, and it was hot outside. A replay of my last flight would do me in. I groaned as a flight crew directed the passengers to a C-130 sitting on the tarmac. We filed in and I was pleased to see there were seats for everyone at the very least. But it was suffocatingly hot inside the plane. Nausea and mild panic swept over me. Suddenly, hitchhiking up Highway 1 seemed like a reasonable and pleasant alternative to flying. I preemptively took my kit off and rolled up my sleeves. If I did throw up I would have my helmet ready for the express purpose. The flight crew was busy making sure the passengers and their gear were loaded up. A female Air Force Captain came down the narrow stairs out of the cockpit and walked over to where I was fumbling with my seatbelt.

"Hey, do you wanna ride up in the cockpit?" she asked, removing her headset. I nearly shouted yes. "Take your weapon but leave all the rest of your stuff here." Sweet Jesus, I was saved.

I followed the Captain up into the cockpit, and immediately felt the life-giving cool of high-powered air conditioning steep into my sweaty uniform, soothing my flushed skin. It was quiet in the cockpit, insulated from the deafening racket only a C-130 can make. I could practically hear angels singing the hallelujah chorus around me. The

144

pilot directed me to buckle in to a bench seat at the rear of the small cockpit and the Captain took her seat behind the plane's navigation equipment.

We took off shortly, leaving the desolate brown of Uruzgan far below us. Snowy mountains appeared out the large front window. You could see everything from up there. My rescuer turned to me from her station and motioned me to stand up. The co-pilot pointed me to a handle just behind the left side of the pilot's head, and I grabbed on. In a flash he pulled up on the controls, sending the plane skyrocketing for a few seconds, making my knees buckle under me until I was practically squatting from the force. Under his aviator sunglasses I could see his left eye wrinkling. He was laughing.

"Hold on!" he said, dropping the nose of the plane back down, practically sending me crashing into the ceiling. My stomach dropped. This time *I* laughed. The smiling navigator motioned for me to sit back down and buckle up.

They were beginning their landing cycle. Soon, the mountains disappeared into lush green farmland, and the sprawling city of Bagram appeared on the horizon. Before long, we were safely on the ground.

Chapter 18

Out of the Wreck

The CST manager, Maria, met me at the passenger terminal and drove me across the massive NATO base to the small Special Operations compound. She dropped me at the female transient quarters and I claimed a bottom bunk, preparing to settle in to my fourth home in a month. Then, she gave me the news that I had been dreading to hear – even though my name was cleared at the SOTF-E level, the commander of the overall Special Operations task force in Afghanistan, a two-star general, was responsible for making the final determination about my situation. Commander Harrison had sent a scathing cover letter with my investigation packet to Maj. Gen. Kent, the commander, outlining my leadership failures. Additionally, he had contacted Aaron and Dan in Shajoy, requesting sworn statements about my behavior. Aaron wrote that our operational difficulties weren't my fault – Shajoy was a district on lockdown. He didn't witness any inappropriate behavior from me, but admitted my and Haley's presence was a distraction to his team of men. Dan wrote that I was more concerned with my own vanity than furthering the ODA mission, and was lazy and non-contributing.

Consequently, Maj. Gen. Kent and his staff wanted to send me home with a negative evaluation report and letter of reprimand, both of which were career-enders and would go in my permanent file. Legally, he wasn't allowed to hold my investigation against me, since it was proved to be groundless. However, if he could demonstrate that I had grossly failed as a leader, he could rightfully send me packing and mar my record. The news devastated me. This couldn't be the end. *"God,"* I pleaded silently, *"If You're still fighting for me, now would be a really great time to speak up."*

The next week felt like a replay of the several weeks prior: eat, sleep, work out and wait for people echelons above my pay grade to decide my future. After a while, the realization sunk in. *This really could be the end of the road for my career.* I finally made peace with my circumstances, mid-workout one mild evening. Katy Perry's song, *Wide Awake*, was on repeat on my iPod while I did pull-ups on a shaky bar outside the gym in the dark. I mentally surrendered to whatever was to come, finally seeing everything with clear eyes. I had been battling my circumstances like a wounded fighter without a weapon. So quickly I had forgotten my battle for victory was not against flesh and blood. The people I marked as my enemies (Haley, the ODA in Shajoy and Cdr. Harrison) were *not* my adversaries. My grandma was right, the true enemy had spread the curse of shame and accusation and fear. It had poisoned people's minds against me, keeping them from seeing the truth. It had even diseased my *own mind* against me, causing me to question my capabilities and also the very essence of my faith! I had let broken people tell me who I was, not the Lord of Heaven's Armies, who had anointed my life with a bold calling and led me into battle. That calling didn't change, even when life around me was falling apart. He held each piece in his hand and had the power to redeem and restore it. He had done it before and would do it again.

Days later, without explanation, my investigation was dropped. Maj. Gen. Kent and his staff suddenly dismissed their case against me, allowing me to continue working, without any black marks on my record. They also approved the CST women to take 15 days of mid-tour leave, effective immediately, after preemptively extending our deployment past Thanksgiving. Maria gave me the good news on June 17. On June 19, I was on my way to Kuwait for a flight home for R&R.

A few days later I sat in front of a computer on Camp Arifjan, waiting for a flight home, trying my best to make sense of the last four months of my deployment. Objectively, I should have been grateful that I had survived with my career and sanity intact – and I was! If there had been a prize for enduring hardship, I would have won the gold medal. But four months of gaping nothingness haunted me. My expectations had been *so* high yet I had done so little. I felt cheated and bitter, desperate to make sense of it all. So, I sat down to type an update to my family and friends, knowing the clarity would come when I started writing.

On Failure, Futility and the Future

Well, here I am at month four, and what a month it has been! I alluded to some of my frustrations and struggles in my last update letter. Since I believe in being transparent with the people in my life and sharing my experiences (because experience truly is the best teacher), I'll share a little more candidly with you all.

As I wrote in my last update, my partner and I left our operating site, bound for a new team. The move was not under good circumstances in many regards. My teammate, who I had trusted with my life, figuratively and literally, started a whirlwind of accusations against me, bringing her gripes directly to our higher headquarters without my knowledge. She claimed I was mentally unstable, made false statements and threw temper tantrums, and generally conducted myself in an unprofessional manner. Consequently, I went under investigation for fraternization and conduct unbecoming an officer, which was brought to the attention of the commanding general in charge of all special operations in Afghanistan. Just like David facing Goliath.

After a couple excruciating weeks, the investigation was dropped due to a lack of substantiated evidence. However, the witch hunt continued. Our team sergeant's accusations that I had been responsible for the failure of the CST out at our previous site crept up our chain of command. In my second letter, I expounded a bit on our never-ending struggles to engage the female portion of the very traditional Islamic population—perhaps the most conservative area in all of Afghanistan. It seemed like we were set up for failure from the beginning. But, part of the burden of being a leader is bearing the weight of failure and success of your subordinates, and being prepared to answer at all times for your decisions and actions.

Realistically, I cannot be held responsible for hundreds of years of deeply rooted culture, which disallows women to do anything aside from produce offspring and prepare meals. And reaching out to the male portion of the population was just as futile. If they regard their flock of goats as higher in value than their wives and daughters, what is going to make them take me, the heathen blond-haired blue-eyed demon from America, seriously?

Regardless, some high-ranking people involved in the situation drank the "poisoned water," as my dad put it, and began to question my competency and leadership, and consequently, wanted nothing more than to send me back home with a bad evaluation and letter of reprimand. I can honestly say that looking the end of my Army career straight in the face was one of the most humbling (humiliating?) and frightening things I could imagine. It's unbelievable how a little spark can start such a wildfire.

I tell you these things to set the stage for the next chain of events and the lessons that I learned, not to make you pity me or despise my partner. After a month stuck in a miserable purgatory of waiting for people way above me to make decisions, I finally made peace with my circumstances and mentally surrendered to whatever was to come. In those moments, I learned some valuable lessons. And though learned in the context of deployment, they transcend into all areas of life:

1. This is not the end of the road for me – this deployment is a rung in the ladder of my life and doesn't determine my future (thanks, mom). I joined the CST program with big aspirations and worked hard to make the cut, because it was something I truly believed in and saw myself being successful in it. Though my dreams have been tempered by disappointment and perceived failure, it's not the end of the road. I will walk away from this deployment with a tarnished reputation and no taste of glory, but I will walk away as an infinitely stronger, wiser and appreciative person. No accolades could ever make up for that.

2. Always consider the source. Over the last few years, this bit of wisdom is something that my dad has imparted in me time and time again when I come under attack (it happens frequently – I have a lot of haters). One NCO I met put it well when he asked, "If a 10 year old tells you you're stupid and ugly, are you going to believe him? No. So why would you believe these people when they tell you you're a failure?" There will always be people who live to see the demise of others. Don't let them get a vote.

Three days ago, the witch hunt ended. I don't know why or how, but I was told that my slate was clean, and that I would be able to go to a new site, with a new teammate to operate for the remainder of the deployment. I believe things happen for a reason, if we let ourselves see the significance of our circumstances.

3. Which brings me to my last lesson. Things happen in their own time. This seems vague, but I believe that nothing happens apart from God's understanding (though life seems a mystery to me much of the time) and things fall into place the way they are supposed to, at the right time. However, that isn't an excuse for us to do nothing and wait for the stars to align, but more as a reason to have patience. Tiny seeds don't turn into flowers overnight and the results of our work don't instantly manifest themselves, but they will if we have the time to wait.

So, this closes a frustrating, agonizing life chapter, forging a new, hopeful future for me. As Florence and the Machine put it, "the dog days are over." I'm happy to report that as I write this, I'm in Kuwait waiting for a plane to take me home to my family and friends for 15 glorious days of R&R. Our deployment has been extended and its turned out to be a blessing. The timing is perfect, and I look forward to the comforts of home and being around people who love me the most. Thank you again for all your support from home. It's an honor to have the support of such incredible people. Hopefully I will get to see and thank many of you in person. I can't tell you what strength and encouragement I gain from you all every day, especially my wonderful family.

Love and hugs from the desert,

Meredith

Chapter 19

True North

My jetlagged and somewhat smelly (from 18 hours on a plane) self was welcomed at the airport near my parents' house by an entourage of enthusiastic family members and friends holding handmade signs and balloons. After a whirlwind of hugs and tears all around, I went home for a meager four hours of sleep before boarding another plane and heading to Florida with my parents to watch my 16-year-old sister Madeline play in a national volleyball tournament. I spent much of that first week in a state of mild culture shock and crowd paranoia, but was eventually able to relax and enjoy the time with my family.

After returning to Illinois to hotter-than-Afghanistan temperatures, I enjoyed my final week with a full house of family. My sister Lydia flew in from southern California and my younger sister Laura drove from Indiana to join in our 4th of July festivities. During the day, with Madeline out of school and my cousin Tristan visiting from Missouri, I was youthfully kept busy playing tennis, running through sprinklers and splashing through the fountains at a local park. It was nice to forget for a while that I was a responsible adult with a heavy burden to carry and let myself be carefree – something I hadn't experienced in quite some time.

While out shopping with some of the ladies in my family one day, Lydia and I came across a sign that read, *Home is Where Mom Is*. We both laughed knowingly. With the exception of Madeline, who is still in high school, my sisters and I were all fiercely independent and adventurous, making our homes far, far away from where we grew up.

Being back in Illinois for two weeks got me thinking about the concept of home and everything that the word embodies. There are magazines and television shows dedicated to help to help you make yours more modern, more southern, more comfortable, more valuable, and more, well, *whatever you want it to be*. Without a doubt, Americans are mildly obsessed with *home*. Sentimentally speaking, home is so much more to most people than a place to lay your head every night. It implies safety, rest and physical and emotional shelter.

So what does home mean to me, a soldier whose lifestyle was based around residential instability? I've laid my head at night in some pretty interesting and sometimes undesirable places: inside armored vehicles, out in the woods in the shelter of trees, in the open desert under the stars, in metal shipping containers, on a variety of Army-issue cots, mud huts, countless prison-style bunks with questionable mattresses, on aircraft, in folding chairs, on floors under desks, and flopped on top of rucksacks. How do I possibly find any sense of home and stability in a combat zone, 7,000 miles from the life I know?

Well, one thing I discovered, especially in the midst of times of isolation and struggle, is that home is a feeling I take with me. It's the memories of better times and moments of love and beauty that create a little anchor in my heart that keep the loneliness and fear from rising. Those feelings tend to visit me in the night, when my mind has freedom to wander. To quell the ache, it helps to think back to things like the way the birds sound on an early summer morning or watching a humid thunderstorm from the front porch. Instead of wistful longing, I turn the memories of happiness and comfort into a sort of emotional safety net – a way to keep myself from giving in to negative feelings that threaten to overwhelm me. *Home* is always with me. Showers, a soft bed and being surrounded by people that loved me for two weeks had filled my tank and made me ready to face the last five months of deployment, whatever it would bring.

⚏

I arrived back at Bagram in mid-July, with my nights and days backwards after several days in transit, more than ready to find out my new assignment. Maria briefed me on a developing situation. A CST operating in Eastern Afghanistan had been having interpersonal issues and was going to be split up and reassigned elsewhere. I would be joining Lynn, an Army 1st Lieutenant and current team leader, in

Paktika Province. I had met her teammate, Michele, in Bagram a few weeks earlier on my way home for R&R. She told me she and Lynn weren't getting along, and that Lynn had been the source of conflict within the partnership. Michele was at the end of her rope and requested a new teammate. I was the first pick to be paired with Lynn. Whether it was out of convenience or punishment, I wasn't sure. At that point I was in no position to ask questions or make demands.

Within a few short days I found myself on a small civilian contractor's airplane, flying peacefully away from Bagram into Paktika Province. I tried to remember Lynn from the training course. Had we ever talked? I didn't think so. She had been on the first team, part of the group of gazelles who could run two miles in less time than it took me to get out of bed in the mornings. I couldn't recall any details about her other than the view of the back of her strawberry blonde head four rows in front of me.

"Lord, please help me endure whatever craziness is to come," I prayed. "I don't think I can handle more conflict."

The plane touched down smoothly on the runway at FOB Sharana as the sun was getting low in the sky. A gruff Green Beret from the AOB came to pick me up, less than pleased with chauffeur duty. He drove me, gear in tow, to their gated compound, a tidy complex of hardstand buildings with tin roofs and a small motor pool. The AOB commander, a tanned, slick-haired Green Beret named Major Randall greeted us outside the TOC building. Upon closer inspection, I saw that *all* the Green Berets walking around the compound were unnaturally tan and had meticulously styled hair, which was just long enough to fall outside of Army regulations. Most of them wore short silky shorts and flip-flops, shirts optional. Outside the gates of the compound, the rest of the regular Army units on the FOB followed strict uniform standards and carried unloaded weapons at the low ready at all times. Being elite came with certain privileges and dressing like they were on vacation in a combat zone was one of them.

"We have designated daily tanning time," Maj. Randall said with a too-white smile, gesturing to several cots hidden behind the operations center. "We call it our daily synch meeting."

That explained why his team guys looked like oiled-up Malibu Ken dolls. They probably shared a giant vat of hair pomade, too, I mused. Maj. Randall showed me around the small compound, where I would be for the next day or so. There were laundry machines, running water, a movie room with a large flat screen TV and wireless Internet. There was a dining facility within walking distance outside the compound. He explained that the new ODA would arrive in a couple days to pick up supplies and bring me back to their VSP in Sar Howza district, wherever that was. He would call the team leader and let him know I had arrived. Until then, I had nothing to do but kill time.

After a late dinner in the nearby dining facility, I unpacked my green sleeping bag and spread it over the respectable looking twin mattress on the bed I had claimed. There were beds for six people in the transient quarters, but I was the only visitor currently it seemed. Despite my exhaustion, I was still too jetlagged to sleep, betrayed by my internal clock, which was scrambled from travel. I felt familiar dark, panicky loneliness start to set in as I lay on the bed, listening to the hum of generators outside. I grasped for some sort of anchor to keep my quickly blooming anxiety from rising to the surface. I suddenly remembered the wireless Internet, and spent nearly an hour futilely trying to connect to the network so I could contact my family. It would be morning there. Much to my dismay, the Internet appeared to be down for the time being. I felt crushed and alone.

I'd always had trouble getting my bearings in a new place, even as I was a kid. I left more sleepovers early than I can count, getting homesick after only a few hours away. Middle-of-the-night panic attacks were common anytime I woke up in a new place, unable to immediately figure out where I was. Traveling away from home always made me feel unsettled, and not in a bold, adventurous way. I craved stability and familiarity, especially here, where meaningful human connection was the exception and conflict was the rule of the land. Even as an adult, I hadn't gotten used to being constantly uprooted. It made my compass spin.

I tried to find my little piece of home in my mind, knowing God had not simply *asked* me to be strong and courageous, but *commanded* me to[17]. He was with me wherever I went, before me and behind me.

---

[17] Joshua 1:9

He was my true north, my horizon line, especially when I struggled to get my legs underneath me. Eventually my fatigue took over and I fell into a dreamless asleep.

The next day, I putted around the small compound, trying to stay out of the way. The TOC was small and every workstation was filled. Even though the team appeared to be made up of a bunch of dandies, they had serious work to do. Their area of responsibility was kinetic, and the ODAs on the ground were working hard and spread thin. The team coming to pick me up was really only half of an ODA. The other half was several miles away from Sar Howza in Orgun district, operating independently. There was a lot of work to do, and they were undermanned significantly.

Later in the afternoon, while I was uselessly wandering around, Maj. Randall stopped me outside the TOC, leaning over the railing of the wooden front porch to talk.

"You're quite the legend around here," he said with a smirk.

"Am I, sir?" I replied with a sigh. I felt suddenly intimidated, despite my amusement with his perfectly pomaded hair and over-bleached teeth.

We talked for a while, the railing separating us. I suspected he was trying to vet me before sending me out with the ODA. I answered his questions about my background politely, skimming over my troubles with Haley when he asked about Shajoy. Honestly I was sick to death of retelling the story to everyone who asked. Maj. Randall was particularly shocked when I told him I'd gone to a private Christian school and earned a degree in art.

"Man, everybody said you're some crazy cheerleader type, partying it up everywhere you go," he said laughing and looking perhaps a little disappointed that I wasn't living up to my legend. "But you seem pretty quiet and shy."

Story of my deployment. The conversation thankfully turned operational, and I eventually made my escape back to my room. I just wanted to get to work and keep my head down until it was time to redeploy. I didn't dare let myself feel anything else. Experience had convinced me I needed to dream small and take up as little space as possible. Believing for big things and wanting more than my fair share had nearly broken me so far. I was afraid to open myself up to

155

possibility again.

That evening, the Internet started working again and I gratefully connected, sending an update to my family. The familiar blue and white of my Facebook homepage comforted me as I scrolled through pictures of new babies, family vacations, weddings and mundane life updates. Life was still happening for my friends and family on the other side of the world at a predictable pace, and that reassured me.

Chapter 20

All Things New

I walked out of my temporary quarters the next morning to see the ODA convoy had arrived along with a small squad of infantry soldiers as security. The few Green Berets I saw all had scraggly beards, long (by military standards), greasy hair and filthy uniforms. They looked feral. I had heard from Michele that there weren't showers or laundry facilities at the VSP and seeing the guys confirmed the less than pristine living conditions. Maj. Randall found me and introduced me to the team leader, a stout Hawaiian captain named Caleb. Maj. Randall's flawlessly coiffed hair looked somewhat absurd next to Caleb's wild, unwashed mane.

While the AOB team was living a comfortable life with hot showers and flushing toilets and designated tanning time each afternoon, Caleb and his team and the CST had been living in primitive conditions out in a remote Afghan village, with limited resources and support. I chuckled to myself at the contrast and looked forward to getting my boots dirty again.

Caleb was warm and friendly and we chatted in the shade of a nearby building while the rest of his team did laundry, showered and picked up packages sent from home. At least outwardly he seemed to take interest in what skills and experience I could offer his team, and even voiced his support for the CST initiative. I was skeptical, but chose to give him the benefit of the doubt. After all, no other man I had worked for up to that time seemed anything but leery of having women in their midst. All I wanted to do was to get to work and finish the deployment with at least a shred of my dignity intact. Who knew what rumors or truth Caleb and his team had heard about me. I was so used to being fodder for gossip that part of me didn't care anymore. Whether they liked me or not didn't particularly matter. But man, I really hoped

Lynn wasn't going make my life hell.

Caleb introduced me to Drew, a quiet and wiry blonde intelligence specialist, and Chris, a weapons specialist with a beard so massive that it completely hid his face and neck. The rest of his Green Berets were at the VSP with Lynn. After a few hours of waiting around while the team completed their hygiene and resupply routine, it was finally time to leave the base and head to the VSP. The Humvee I was assigned to ride in for the hour-long trip only had two seats up front for Caleb and his driver, a young infantry private. I sat in the open back behind an M249 machine gun mounted to one side of the vehicle, next to the infantry squad leader, who was sporting impressive tan lines from his protective eyewear.

As we left the base through the controlled maze of barriers and guards, I began to feel inexplicably happy and optimistic about the days to come. Nothing had indicated that this go-round would be better. I expected a challenge working with Lynn, though not of Haley caliber. The weather was warm and overcast as the convoy navigated the winding, climbing roads to Sar Howza. The landscape was beautiful, in its own desolate way. The paved road wound through gently rolling hills, covered with low scrubby brush and the occasional apricot orchard. Ancient looking mountains stood on the far edges of the horizon. The scenery was reminiscent of the American Southwest.

As we drove out through the wilderness, I kept expecting the feeling of intense loneliness that had been so pervasive during the last few months to overtake me, but it never did. I felt different, like the burden I had been carrying with me had evaporated and I was left with just me – the confident and capable captain who had been hidden away since February. I cherished the feeling as we finished the drive through the mud village to the VSP. The paved road soon turned into dirt and mud houses lined the rudimentary path, which was filled with deep ruts made by rain and armored vehicle traffic. Raw sewage and wastewater flowed out of holes in the bottom of compound walls and into the street. Hordes of young children, mainly boys, chased after our convoy, screaming for water, which seemed to be the only English word they knew.

"Wat*ah*! Wat*ah*!" they demanded in chorus with outstretched arms. Even in plastic sandals they were quick and agile.

Small girls eyed us warily from the edges of the road. They were dressed in every shade of the rainbow, their dark heads covered in glittering scarves. Their hands, stained orange with henna, occasionally reached out towards us to beg for whatever we might give them. Even some of the smallest girls held grubby, half-dressed babies on their hips. Their big kohl-lined eyes stared through us.

The convoy drove past the outer edge of the village and continued beyond an Afghan Local Police checkpoint. The men in the guard tower gave us friendly waves as we passed. The lead vehicle turned off onto a dusty side road, which led to a small compound surrounded by a tall stone and mortar wall. One by one the vehicles pulled into the camp through an opening in the wall, which was guarded by an armored vehicle. Sitting at nearly 9,000 feet the camp was austere in every sense of the word. A few portable toilets and some sad looking plywood structures haphazardly lined the inner walls. A jagged mountain range to the immediate north formed a formidable wall between the VSP and a neighboring village. The camp was raw and dirty, exposed to the elements.

Lynn smiled and waved from a guard tower in the far corner. Her uniform pants and shirt were covered in dirt, but she looked happy. I smiled and watched her climb down the ladder from the tower. She wrapped me up in a hug as I dismounted from the truck, giving me a hearty "How are ya?" before I could even take my body armor off. She seemed genuinely excited to see me. With a pang of conviction, I remembered that I, of all people, should have known not to judge others based on rumors. I knew I hadn't given her the same benefit of the doubt that I expected other people to give to me. Another lesson learned. Lynn was friendly and talkative as she gave me the grand tour of the small camp and introduced me to the rest of the ODA.

Justin and Mark were two medics assigned to the team. Justin was fresh out of the Special Forces medic course and had arrived just a few days before me. Mark had been temporarily pulled from another team to cover medical support until Justin got up to speed. Next, I met Josh, the team's engineer. Alex, the communications specialist, was on leave, and Caleb showed me pictures of him with his new baby girl. A small squad of Army infantry soldiers supplemented the small ODA. Doug, an Army canine handler, and Schester, his sweet but lethal

Belgian Malinois rounded out the small crew on the VSP. They were a calm group for the most part, and at least outwardly harbored no prejudice against having women around.

The CST living quarters were underneath the guard tower, with makeshift walls made out of rock-filled Hesco barriers and a ceiling crudely constructed of sandbag and tarp-covered plywood. It served as a bunker in the event of an attack, being the only somewhat bulletproof structure on the small camp. The door to the bunker was a bed sheet strung across a piece of rope. Inside, the ground was covered with flooring made of plywood and two-by-four planks. The heads of three cots were pushed up against the wall in a neat line. Someone had routed a long power cord off the main generator so there was enough electricity to power a couple bare light bulbs hanging on the walls. Someone had also strung a collection of headscarves in a colorful array across a bungee cord rigged to one of the Hesco walls. It was crude and dirty, but somehow looked homey. The CST's interpreter, a Pakistani-American Pashtun from Long Island, greeted me warmly while I moved my belongings inside. Her name was Meena – a gentle, soft-spoken woman in her early fifties who wore a traditional hijab. She had been in Afghanistan for nearly a year, working with other CST women prior to joining Lynn and Michele. She spoke and read multiple languages and was a devout Muslim.

A team of specially trained Afghan police shared the compound with the ODA. The Special Squad was part of an elite force under the leadership of the infamous Commander Azizullah, a controversial and legendary military figure in southeastern Afghanistan. Special Squad and the ODA worked and lived side by side to promote peace and stability in the district and root out insurgency. Our Afghan partners were perpetually hospitable and friendly. Meena had become a mother figure to them, scolding them in Pashto when they became too rowdy and offering them kind words of encouragement. In return, they revered and honored her, making her tea every morning and ensuring she wanted for nothing.

Chapter 21

Two in the Heart, One in the Mind

Lynn and I became fast friends and the remainder of the summer passed quickly at the VSP. She was big-hearted and intelligent and had a penchant for practical jokes. She was the kind of person that didn't wait for you to ask her for help – she was always in the thick of things anytime there was work to do. Lynn was a loyal friend who would also good-naturedly heckle you to no end when you messed up. Her carefree joy and easygoing disposition rubbed off on me and I felt myself coming back to life, leaving behind the disappointment of the last several months. Our partnership blossomed as we planned and strategized together. We didn't agree 100 percent of the time, but our disagreements only drove us to be better. Our mutual respect and unconditional support paved the way for us to be successful and to have a lot of fun in the meantime.

On slow days, Lynn and I watched episode after episode of *Glee* in our bunker, my laptop open on the tough box between our cots. She would often sing along to the songs, with a voice she once described as *garbage cans rolling over cats*. The men on the team, whose living quarters were on the backside of our bunker, would yell over the Hesco barriers for Lynn to quiet down, which only made her sing more. They began jokingly calling her *American Idol*. She was awkward and endearing, smart and hard working. I couldn't help but adore her and be incredibly grateful for her partnership.

Lynn and I kept a curious eye on Haley via our weekly video conferences and through social media, watching to see if she was continuing to leave a trail of disasters in her wake. Haley had long blocked me from viewing her Facebook page, but she and Lynn were still connected. One evening Lynn called me to the computer where she was checking her email and catching up on social media. Plastered on

Haley's page were pictures of her and an Army sergeant she had met at her new VSP and was now dating. She announced they were moving in together upon their return to the states and virtually picking out furniture online. I couldn't believe was I was seeing – an officer, who had falsely accused me of fraternization, was in a relationship with an enlisted man – the very thing she had accused me of. Hot, angry tears poured out of my eyes as Lynn and I sat shoulder to shoulder on a wooden bench, shocked and horrified at what we were witnessing.

Anger rolled over me in wave after wave. I couldn't make sense of her blatant hypocrisy and wanted nothing more than to watch Haley's career burn to the ground. Lynn took screenshots of the posts and sent them to Maria, our CST manager, demanding that something be done immediately. Maria wrote back shortly. *There's been way too much drama this deployment already. If I bring it up to the task force commander we will all look bad. Just keep your heads down and finish out the deployment.* I wept for hours that night, unable to make sense of anything. At a deep level I craved vindication, but it never came. A few days later while on the phone with my youngest sister, Madeline, she spoke wise words beyond her 16 years.

"It sounds like Haley is a really unhappy person and must live a miserable life," her small voice said on the distant end of the phone. It finally sunk in – even though there would be no justice for her behavior, Haley paid dearly for it every day: in broken relationships, constant dissatisfaction, mistrust, and hollow, isolating superiority. I knew I had to let go of my bitterness or it was going to poison me.

Caleb and his small team embraced us as sisters, bringing us along on nearly every foot patrol and convoy to the village and teasing us mercilessly around camp. They collectively admitted that they detested Haley more than their ex-wives, and taught me how to throw a real punch and fight with a knife, just in case we had a confrontation at the end of deployment.

The team wholeheartedly believed they could accomplish their stability mission better with us than without us. Their faith in our capabilities opened doors for us to operate in an unhindered capacity. The ODA never questioned or doubted our decisions and frequently gave us ample time and opportunity to run with a lead or explore a new effort when we thought it would be worthwhile. It was glorious. Their support was incredibly freeing and motivated us to do even better work.

Most of our missions with the ODA that summer involved walking or driving into the village of Sar Howza and talking with locals in the bazaar or on the streets. Hordes of dusty, boisterous children would gather around Lynn and I, fascinated by the blonde soldier women wearing headscarves. Our presence usually served to distract the crowds of unruly kids so that the team could talk to village elders or police checkpoint commanders unhindered. We usually stuffed our cargo pockets full of snacks to hand out, often in exchange for information about Taliban activity in the village. It worked brilliantly. Kids were the best source of intelligence in Sar Howza. They saw everything that happened within their homes and would often blurt out the truth with unfiltered honesty.

On one mission in mid-summer, a particularly large crowd of young boys had gathered around Lynn and I, screaming *Pin! Pin!* with outstretched hands, knowing we frequently carried cheap ballpoint pens to hand out. Through Meena, we asked them if they knew anything about a Taliban commander in the village, whom the team suspected lived nearby. Instantly, several older kids pointed to a younger boy.

"His father is the Taliban commander!" they excitedly told us in Pashto, giving us the commander's full name and pointing out his house. They knew honesty was rewarded with American goodies.

The small boy looked bewildered to suddenly have his family exposed, but agreed quietly and said, "Yes, he is. But he's not here right now. He's in Pakistan and will be back in September."

Meena took him off to the side and told him what a good boy he was, giving him extra candy and pens for his confession.

One hot afternoon during a foot patrol into the village bazaar, Lynn and Meena and I were doing our usual crowd control tactics, rounding up rowdy boys and quizzing them on what English words they knew, and if they could name any U.S. presidents. It was a fun game that kept them occupied and also let us break the ice with a dozen or so kids at once.

"Who's the president of the United States?" Lynn asked the crowd.

"Hilary Clinton!" one child shouted back.

"George Bush!" yelled another.

"Na, na[18], Barack Obama!" an older child cut in authoritatively.

A young man in traditional dress, appearing in his early twenties, approached the group and addressed me. Lynn had moved on to teaching a kid how to blow bubbles, and he was spitting all over her hand trying to get a hang of it.

"Hello, how are you?" the man asked. It wasn't uncommon for locals to know very basic English greetings from primary school.

"Fine, how are you?" I replied, not expecting an answer. The locals didn't usually speak enough English to say more than hello. I was distracted by Lynn's unsanitary bubble blowing endeavor and Meena wasn't around to interpret for me. I assumed he would practice his few English words and continue on his way.

"I'm doing very well, thank you," he said in perfect English.

"Wait, do you speak English?" I asked, surprised, whipping my head back around to look at him.

"Yes! I live in New York City," he said proudly.

My jaw dropped. Overhearing this exchange, Lynn stopped mid-bubble and grilled the man on how he came to live in the states and what he was doing in Sar Howza. The man explained that he had returned to his home village from New York City to get married and bring his new wife back to the U.S. His family owned a KFC franchise in the city. We talked a few minutes longer, flabbergasted by the chance encounter. Sar Howza was remote and relatively primitive. Running into an educated English speaker and American resident there didn't register on the list of things to expect. Lynn and I laughed, wondering at the odds, the rest of the afternoon.

Life at the VSP was as unglamorous and simple as it could be. There was no running water and we were perpetually dirty. The food was awful, with the exception of what our Afghan partners brought us out of kindness and pity. Rats the size of cats (and actual cats) visited our bunker at night while we slept. We would wake up to the sound of rattling floorboards, and in the moonlight witness a scurrying shadow at our feet. Sudden light from our headlamps would send the rats running back for the door. The cats, which unfortunately did nothing for our rat

---

[18] Means "no, no" in Pashto

problem, would climb into the Hesco barriers above our heads and find a gap underneath the plywood ceiling. There, they would howl eerily for several hours before moving on.

Despite living in relative squalor, I was inexplicably joyful. After so many weeks of turmoil and suffering, God began to pour out His sudden blessings on my weary head. He redeemed my life from the grave and have me solid ground to stand on. He brought healing friendships and fresh success into my path. At first I was in disbelief, waiting for the ground to drop out underneath me. But, God continued to show me grace and favor as I embraced His goodness with a thankful heart.

⁂

Warm summer days in the mountains faded majestically into cool, clear nights. Each person on the camp was responsible for a two-hour guard shift between dusk and first light every night. After the last of the evening sun faded to a velvety blue, a breathtaking sky full of constellations would appear. The VSP was so isolated that there wasn't a city with electricity for miles. With virtually no light pollution, the haze of the Milky Way was brightly visible. I found indescribable peace every night sitting in the tower, covered with a glittering veil of stars, the mountain in front of me standing stalwart against the inky sky. The Perseid Meteor Shower peaked mid-summer and the sky rained down stars for hours on end. I selfishly drank in the beauty as if nature was putting on a show just for me.

That year, the Muslim Ramadan fell mid-summer. Special Squad and the interpreters on the VSP, including Meena, fasted from first light to sundown, not even taking a sip of water or bite of food, despite frequent daytime patrols in the heat of the afternoon. At night, as the sun began to set, the camp would come alive as the Afghans prepared food to break the fast and blasted traditional music from small plastic radios. All their food came from the local bazaar and included an array of fresh apricots, almonds, mangos, grapes, and melons. Each night they would offer their American partners paper trays full of fruits and steaming rice, knowing our standard Army rations consisted of little more than frozen burritos and chicken fingers day after day. Lynn,

Meena and I would eagerly devour our feast sitting on tough boxes inside the bunker, enjoying the cool stillness of the end of the day in the dim glow of our bare light bulbs.

One golden evening toward the end of the summer, Caleb climbed up the ladder to the guard tower where I had just started my two-hour block of duty. We talked for a while, looking out onto the mountain in the waning light. We talked about my previous struggles in Zabul with both the ODA and Haley and how I had come to his team feeling defeated.

"You know, you and Lynn are the task force's biggest success story," he said. "People are talking about you all the way up the chain of command to Maj. Gen. Kent."

"Really?" I asked in disbelief. Mere weeks earlier Kent had wanted to send me home.

He smiled and nodded. "Your success is the best revenge you could ever have against anyone who didn't believe in you."

After he left, tears formed in the corners of my eyes, and for the first time since I'd arrived in Afghanistan, they weren't tears of fear or anger. They were pure tears coming from a full heart. God had done the impossible, setting my feet on a rock high above the heads of my enemies. I quietly thanked Him for His goodness and mercy, feeling overwhelmed with gratitude for His faithfulness.

One morning after breakfast, I went and checked my email in the 20-foot metal shipping container that served as an operations center. As I was finishing up, a loud explosion caught everyone's attention. Explosion sounds were not entirely unusual in our area, as a group of local workers frequently blasted their way through the mountain north of the VSP to build a road. I went outside just as another explosion erupted nearby, about 150 meters outside the compound wall. The smoke and dirt rose skyward from the ground at the place of impact. People began to speculate that either a mine or IED had just been triggered and everyone started climbing on top of armored vehicles and guard towers for a better view. Immediately we heard the telltale whistle of a mortar just as one hit the ground no farther than 100 meters from the camp. We realized the VSP was receiving indirect fire. Whoever was firing was walking the mortars into our VSP, dialing in their aim with every subsequent launch. Then, a fourth round impacted 25 meters away from our northwest wall, sending everyone on the camp scrambling for body armor and weapons. The bunker was the only safe place, but even a direct hit from a mortar would still blow the roof right off.

I ushered Meena into the bunker, telling her to put her kit on and stay put. Lynn and I threw on our protective gear and climbed into the guard tower above the bunker. We were still in flip-flops and shorts under our body armor. My heart was racing, knowing the insurgents could easily have dialed their next mortar right into the VSP. A few of the infantry soldiers met us in the tower, chomping at the bit to shoot someone. Lynn and I grabbed the binoculars and high-powered scope that were kept in the tower and began scanning the mountains for spotters. After several minutes I zeroed in on a man at the top of a ridgeline to the northeast, about 1200 meters away. He was dressed in all black, the trail of his turban streaming behind him in the wind. The infantry squad leader trained the sniper rifle on his position. The man popped up and down a few times before disappearing again.

Caleb and the ODA geared up for a dismounted patrol set for the ridge line, hoping to either provoke an attack or send the enemy squirting out of their positions. They returned two hours later, somewhat disappointed after not finding anyone. The VSP didn't receive any more fire after that. We knew an ODA versus anyone would not have been a fair fight. But, the apparent unrest was a good sign. It meant that we were doing something right in the villages. You can't influence change without provoking some unrest from the enemy.

Chapter 22

Upgrade

The summer nights began to turn chilly by mid-August, and Caleb made the decision to move the camp to a more permanent and weatherproof location inside the village before fall brought sub-freezing temperatures to the mountains. We were already spending our guard duty shifts bundled in fleece jackets and caps, wrapping up in poncho liners to keep the chill out. An American infantry company had occupied a compound adjacent to the Sar Howza District Center, and there was room for our crew, including Special Squad, to move into rundown but habitable buildings. The District Center had running water and a dining facility with much better food than we were eating, which were enough reasons for the team to unanimously support the move. Operationally speaking, it made more sense. The District Center was within walking distance of the bazaar, the city's hub of activity, and gave the team immediate access to district officials for ongoing mentorship programs.

One late night we conducted our last patrol into the village before we were to move to the District Center. The ODA wanted to see what the nighttime vibe was in the village. There were murmurs of Taliban activity and intimidation during the hours of darkness, and a nearby police checkpoint had recently been overrun with insurgents shortly before the midnight hour. We set out under a half moon, our monocular night vision devices making us look like strange insects. The clouds that covered the sky earlier in the evening had dissipated. The lunar glow gave us faint shadows on the ground and helped illuminate our optics. As we trekked into the village, I kept my monocular device flipped up, relying on my human night vision to navigate with the patrol. Night vision devices diminish your depth perception, turning the coordinated into klutzes. I had already stepped into a puddle of something wet with my monocular on. By the smell of it I could guess that it wasn't water.

As we approached the village, a chorus of dogs greeted us. They were everywhere, and announced our path through the garbage-strewn mud streets. Other than the occasional bark from the dogs, it was eerily silent and still, without a hint of breeze. The air was cool and was filled with the smell of human and animal waste, despite the rainstorm earlier in the day. It was hard to distinguish the puddles of water from puddles of filth, so I stuck to dry ground as best as I could. We took a narrow lane between compounds into the heart of the village. Next to me, a half-opened metal gate creaked open and closed, despite the still air. It struck me as one of those cliché moments you might see in a creepy movie. We moved past the local mosque deeper into the village, seeing no movement or sign of life aside from the throngs of stray dogs, which lined our route like parade spectators giving away our position.

The narrow alley eventually widened into a street, and we got ourselves into security positions while some of the ODA and Special Squad went to check out a suspected Taliban compound. From my corner of the street I could hear the sound of someone pounding on the aluminum doors that gated the compound, followed by raised voices. After several minutes of trying to get comfortable kneeling on the rocky ground, Lynn and I received a radio call that we were needed inside the compound. We quickly moved inside, where Doug and Schester were searching rooftops and walls for bombs. Caleb told us there was a room of women for us to search and question. Regrettably, we had left Meena at VSP, as she couldn't make the long walk into the village. So, we made do with a male interpreter by having him stand outside the door and translate while we talked to the women.

As we entered the room, it was immediately obvious that everyone inside was frightened. One younger woman was breathing rapidly, distressed by our presence. Another young woman held a small boy, while an older woman looked on. The older woman seemed weary, like she was used to soldiers bursting in on her house in the middle of the night. We removed our helmets to show that we were women, and offered a greeting, letting the women know that we meant them no harm. We searched the women as gently as possible and looked around the room for anything unusual. We questioned them about the Taliban and the safety of their village, trying to glean any information from them that would prove useful. They claimed not to know anything, stating they never left their house, and no visitors ever came in. Lynn and I really couldn't tell if they were lying or not, but I believe they were too terrified to want to tell us much of anything.

We left the house and saw some timid faces poking out of the doorway of an adjacent mud home. We approached the room filled with half a dozen young women and several children, waiting tensely to see if we would come inside their home as well. Lynn dug into her cargo pockets, handing the children candy, which brought tentative smiles to their faces. We broke out the few meager Pashto phrases that we knew, assuring them we were there to help. The women smiled shyly behind their headscarves and waved goodbye as we left.

⚊⚊⚊

By the end of August, shortly before the end of Ramadan, we were set to vacate the VSP. Everyone on the camp worked around the clock to load and move flatbed trailers with all the team's equipment to our new home. Then we made a massive bonfire with the plywood and garbage we couldn't take with us. As the smoke curled up towards the evening sky before our final departure, I felt a little nostalgic about my summer at the VSP. It had been immensely satisfying and healing. I would miss the solitude and beauty of the mountains and the night sky and even our midnight ROUS visits. Life was going to get more comfortable at the DC, but I wasn't ready for how *much* better it was going to be.

At the DC Lynn, Meena and I shared a large room inside the weathered concrete building, which used to be an office complex. We were still sleeping on cots, but we had reliable electricity and a door that closed. Plus, access to hot showers each day and respectable Army fare increased our morale greatly. We also delighted in finding computers with internet access and phones to call home. To top off our excitement, the compound had laundry facilities and a small gym. Mail reached us in an average of eight days from the States, as opposed to the three to four weeks we were used to at the VSP. We were living large!

Shortly after our arrival, the Afghans marked the end of Ramadan, known as Eid al-Fitr, with a day of festivities beginning at sundown. To help celebrate, the District Center and ODA threw a party, inviting several dozen local men, Special Squad and our new American infantry neighbors for an evening of eating and dancing. Caleb, Alex and Drew were good sports, gamely donning traditional shirts, vests and turbans much to the howling delight of Special Squad. With his dark beard and skin, Caleb could easily have passed for a local. Our Afghan partners hired a local four-man band to play traditional music on stringed instruments, drums and a small pump organ.

After a feast of goat[19], naan, a yogurt-mint dipping sauce, and rice, the festivities kicked off. The band set up their instruments on the back of a trailer and played and sang lively music for several hours for the crowd. The Afghan men willingly danced the Attan, the official dance of Afghanistan, in perfect synchronization, around and around in a big circle, song after song. Their steps were flawless and mesmerizing. Occasionally, a brave American would attempt to join in and mimic the twirling steps and claps, much to the delight of all in attendance. Eventually they gave up on learning the complicated dance and either sat back down or spun wildly to their own rhythm. The joyful music and dancing continued into the cool night, finally ending sometime near two in the morning.

Life at the District Center opened up new, vast opportunities for Lynn and I to flex our CST muscles. A small radio station operated out of the District Center compound with equipment donated by an American Civil Affairs team. The DJ, Ahmad, a mild-mannered Afghan man in his early twenties, gave us unlimited permission to contribute content to his show, which mainly played Pakistani and Afghan music and the five daily calls to prayer. Lynn had already left for R&R, but Meena and I wasted no time planning and writing a weekly 30-minute show, which we called *Bibi Hawa*[20].

We crafted the show to target women in the local households,

---

[19] I watched it get slaughtered, so there was no way I was going to eat it

[20] Bibi Hawa means "Miss Eve" in Pashto, essentially a playful nickname amongst women

which we knew would be home, either with other women or their children during the daytime when we chose to air the show. Meena and I created several different segments for the show each week – everything from basic hygiene to prevent disease spread, food and water sanitation, immunization information, cooking tips, and Qur'an verses. I would write the script, and she would translate it into Pashto then record it on a small portable recorder to give to the station. After a Taliban attack or incident in the village, we created pro Afghan Local Police – anti Taliban messages to help quell misinformation campaigns by insurgents. Our greatest measure of success was out in the village, hearing locals excitedly tell us they recognized Meena's voice from her weekly program.

Our success with the radio program drove Lynn and I to work even harder wherever we could find an opportunity. Between missions and meetings with Sar Howza officials at the District Center, time flew by. Before we knew it, September was nearly over. Caleb and his team were due to return home and another ODA was on its way to replace them at the DC. I started to get nervous, wondering how the new team was going to treat Lynn and I. We had accomplished so much as a team in the few short months we had been together and were continuing to gain momentum. Finally, it felt like the work we were doing actually mattered and was making a difference. It was so easy to get sucked into the frustration and seeming futility of Village Stability Operations. But we really believed things were changing, at least slowly. There was talk of and support for a women's shura[21], the first of its kind in the village, and our anti-insurgent messaging seemed to be gaining traction.

But, we knew the incoming ODA would make or break our efforts. They would either support us and let us work or sideline us for our last few months as a team. Caleb, sensing my nervousness about the incoming team, pulled me aside as the small advance party from the new ODA arrived at the camp.

"This is *your* turf. *You're* the expert here, not them. You get to set the pace and show them the ropes. Don't be afraid of them, they're the ones coming into your house. Don't take any s*** from any of

---

[21] A council or gathering, typically organized by local government

them."

I laughed and mentally checked myself. Okay, I had to stop letting myself feel inferior, just because they had Special Forces tabs on their shoulders. Lynn and I weren't any less qualified to do our jobs than they were to do theirs. We had a purpose there and set our minds to continue our success.

Chapter 23

Thankful

Lynn and I said a final goodbye to Caleb and his amazing team. We would miss them, but we didn't have much time to dwell on it. The new team was on ground and ready to get to work. Integrating into their team of 12 went smoother than we anticipated. Ken, the new team leader, was supportive of our roles, as were several of the other men on the team. Still, a few remained skeptical of our presence, but we didn't take it to heart and kept working at the projects we had set in motion.

Each week Lynn, Meena and I met with the District Minister of Education, a former Taliban fighter, and figured out together how to support the local schools and teachers. We also tagged along to various local meetings with the District Governor and other officials. Meena and I continued our radio show and anti-Taliban messaging, and she became somewhat of a local celebrity, especially with our Afghan partners who tuned in each week to hear the show.

Our final two months flew by as we continued to work and support the ODA members, many of whom became brothers to us. We worked side-by-side in the aid station and patrolled into the village together or helped build new structures on the camp, proud to be a contributing part of their team. At night we built bonfires and ate peanut butter cups and drank tea under the stars. Life felt really good, especially with the prospect of going home just around the corner.

In our free time Lynn and I frequented the small dusty gym on the camp, and ran tight circles around the rocky Hesco-lined landing zone, scurrying away from incoming helicopters. At our 7,500 foot elevation we wheezed and complained our way through six workouts a week, while our Afghan partners looked on in disbelief and amusement, thinking we were being punished for bad behavior. We trained for a half marathon together, running like hamsters on a wheel on the small track. Working out gave us a sense of routine and purpose and kept us anchored when we got antsy at the prospect of going home soon.

Eid al-Adha, a Muslim religious festival, fell at the end of October, and once again we threw a lively party for our Afghan partners on the camp to celebrate the occasion. Our young Army cook, John, grilled up a feast for the crowd of Americans and Afghans. After dinner, we danced late into the night to traditional Afghan music blasted from a plastic hand-cranked radio. Special Squad taught us some basic dance moves, which involved spinning and clapping, and we all joined in gleefully. Then, we asked if we could show them some American dance moves, and they excitedly assented. We decided swing dancing was a tame enough dance to introduce to the Afghans, but as soon as Mike, one of the Green Berets, grabbed my hands to dance, Special Squad jumped between us, shouting *no, no, no!* They didn't want any man to touch me, so that quickly put an end to our dance lessons for the night. Soon afterward some of the Afghan interpreters produced henna and asked if they could decorate our hands with traditional designs. Lynn and a few of the more game Green Berets sat with Special Squad in their living quarters while they meticulously painted our hands, passing around a tin of sweets and glass cups of chai. We chatted and teased each other back and forth through the interpreters, enjoying the air of festivity and the camaraderie we had built over the few months of working together. It was near 2:00 a.m. when we finally wrapped up our night of dancing and celebration.

The weather began to turn cold as November arrived. Nighttime temperatures dropped to near freezing each night, and we shivered in our unheated rooms. Only a small square of duct-taped cardboard covered a large hole in the wall above my bed, doing little to keep out the chill. I bundled up under layers of blankets and pulled my fleece cap down tightly over my ears, falling asleep once my body heat warmed my cozy cocoon. Days were sunny and mild, creating a beautiful backdrop for our patrols into the village.

I relished each of our final days, willing my mind to remember how blue the sky was, the dramatic jut of the mountains and how incredible the stars were at night. I was truly grateful to be going home, but I wanted to remember each moment of beauty, like the bustle of the dusty bazaar with its brightly colored shops and the way the curious children chased after us with henna stained hands. Despite the heartbreak of war, there was raw, abundant beauty all around. In some ways I would miss it.

Meena cried as we left and Lynn and I worked hard to fight back tears. She had been a true gift to us. Her motherly kindness and expert skill at translating allowed us to do so much more than we dreamed of in the small village. We were forever indebted to her service to our country. She gave up nearly two years of a comfortable life in the states to work for the U.S. military, knowing the enormous risks of her chosen duty. I would miss Meena dearly. She was a truly exceptional woman.

The convoy dropped us at the AOB on FOB Sharana and Lynn and I made our way to the transient quarters with our bags after saying our goodbyes to the ODA. We claimed two twin beds with mattresses and felt like we'd won the lottery. A flight to Bagram didn't leave until the next afternoon, so we had all the time in the world to enjoy the little luxuries that staying on a large base offered. After hot showers and a decent meal, we wandered through the little Afghan-owned shops nearby, did laundry and used the wireless internet, feeling like giddy kids in a candy store. We said goodbye to the team, having finished their resupply, and watched them pull away from the AOB gate.

It was the day before Thanksgiving, and more than ever I felt there was so much to be thankful for. My heart was full and grateful. We had done our jobs well and all that was left to do was return home. It felt indescribably good to be on our way. Soon, we would be reunited with our CST sisters in Bagram. It didn't even matter that Haley would be there. We were going *home*, for good. Each of our lives had been spared and we would soon be home with our families for Christmas.

The next morning Lynn and I put on fresh uniforms, smelling of Tide and dryer sheets, and rode to the airfield to catch our flight. We grabbed to-go boxes of Thanksgiving lunch knowing we would probably miss dinner in Bagram and shoveled in a few bites before the C-130 landed to pick us up. My heart rose in my chest as the plane accelerated down the runway. I popped my earbuds in and turned on my iPod, smiling at Lynn, as the ground beneath us got smaller. *Goodbye, forever, Paktika*, I thought. Likely I would never see this place again.

We landed earlier than expected, just minutes before the grand

Thanksgiving feast kicked off on the small camp on Bagram where we were staying. We dropped our bags in the large bunk-filled room we would share with the other CSTs and hugged the few women who had arrived before us. Lynn and I made our way to the dining hall feeling ecstatic at the prospect of good food. The Army may serve consistently subpar meals, but they know how to make a solid Thanksgiving dinner. The small dining hall was decked out gaudily in crepe paper turkeys and an array of orange and brown paper decorations declaring *Happy Thanksgiving*! It was cheesy and wonderful at the same time. Smiling cooks filled my brown paper tray with turkey, mashed potatoes, green beans and fresh fruit. The humble meal was the best tasting food I'd ever eaten. I pulled out my small camera and snapped a grainy photo of my tray, trying to capture the feeling of immense gratitude that overwhelmed me. We ate with relish and walked back to our room with full bellies and happy hearts. I said a quick prayer, knowing God understood the sentiments that my words couldn't express adequately. *Thank you, Lord. Thank you for all of it.*

A week later we boarded a commercial airplane bound for the U.S. at Manas Air Base, Kyrgyzstan as thick, heavy flakes of snow began to fall from the night sky. We had only been there for a few hours before a flight opened up for us. The growing blanket of snow outside softened the spartan military structures on the base, lending the surrounding world a calm, still air.

It was almost December, and the magic of the snow ushered in the Christmas season. I tilted my head into the cold sky and contentedly watched my breath turn to clouds against the backdrop of a happy chorus of my sisters' voices. We were going home, together. I wondered if I could feel any happier than that moment. I didn't think so.

Chapter 24

A Package from God

Life in the States gradually returned to calm predictability. In June I would report to the Combined Logistics Captains Career Course at Fort Lee, Virginia, for a six-month long Army course with my peers. I wasn't thrilled about having to stay in the Army for at least two more years, but I had made peace with the inevitability of it. A lot of officers said it was a gentleman's course, which meant it was relatively easy to pass, and there would be ample free time, including weekends off. The Army would give us all our follow-on assignments sometime during the course. So, for the time being, the latter half of the year remained a big blank space.

I rented a house for the five months I would be in Washington and enjoyed the temporary stability. After Christmas I started dating a nice man named Nick and felt like my life was gaining momentum in a positive direction. I returned to my former unit and took on a low-key position as their soldiers trickled back from their own Afghanistan deployment. It was strange being back in the same place I started, under new circumstances, with new eyes. The phases in my life felt like a spiral staircase – cyclical, yet always moving upwards. I frequently found myself in familiar, yet uncharted territory, like each first day of school or watching spring unfold each year. Yet, each vaguely familiar circumstance saw me more learned, calmer, more seasoned, leading me in a progressive journey away from the ground. It's almost as if God offered redemptive opportunities – not a chance to erase the past, but to prove to myself that I could do better than last time.

I spent an evening shortly before my move in a state of jealous frustration after talking on the phone with one of my friends, a man working in Special Forces – a career field limited to only men. He was about to embark on another (what I believed to be) glamorous trip overseas for training. My own military career didn't completely satisfy and I longed for the adventure and excitement that came with his. I was smart, driven, strong and had proven, or so I thought, that I could keep up with elite men like my friend and be an asset to their mission.

But, one hindrance always remained. I was a woman; a woman frequently met with outright hostility from male soldiers. People were incessantly gossiping about whom I might be sleeping around with or how my legs looked in our physical training uniform. As a woman I felt working twice as hard as any man to earn a small fraction of respect was required, though I was extremely professional and great at my job. It was a constant barrage of being treated like a liability and a spectacle, rather than as an asset that warped my mind into believing that my gender really did make me inferior. I wanted so badly to prove them wrong.

In my quest for feminism and demonstrating my worth as a woman in the military, I became just as much of a chauvinist as many of the men that I encountered, who's attitudes toward women I tried so hard to change. I wanted to prove that I could be a part of the mysterious boys' club, and forsook my own gender, denying myself the acknowledgment that I was not a man, and that it was okay that I wasn't. Conflict within myself stirred. I suppressed my expression of feelings and anything aside from logical thought, and made my body a slave to physical fitness, pushing myself to injury and disdaining the appearance of weakness in my own mind and bodily fibers. I condescendingly looked upon other women, especially those who didn't share my same vision of physical eliteness or showed any flicker of human emotion outside of what I considered an acceptable range.

That evening after I hung up the phone with my friend, I went and took a shower, still feeling frustrated. Out of nowhere a seemingly obvious realization hit me square between the eyes: *I'm a woman, and that's okay!* The implications of that realization began to sink in. I felt the Holy Spirit speak gently into my heart as years of backwards thinking washed away. The military culture I had spent much of my formidable young adult life in helped to cultivate the belief that because I was a woman (and obviously therefore a creature filled with unstable emotions, plagued by physical weakness) what I had to offer professionally was less worthy than what a man could offer. With clear eyes I realized that I'd eaten up the lie that being a woman, and all that my gender encompassed, made me inadequate.

As the water of truth washed over me, questions without immediate answers flooded into my mind. Why had I forsaken my own sex, banishing *weaker* women to the dark, icy corners of my heart? Why was I so convinced of my own feminine superiority? And furthermore, how had I convinced myself that what I had to offer to my career, to this vision and calling that God had set before me, was not enough?

Minutes later I found myself weeping to my Creator on the edge of my bed, still wrapped in my damp towel. He spoke loudly into my heart. My usefulness to Him was not dependent on the strength of my physical, mental or emotional self, but on my willingness to say *yes* to His calling on my life. It was not up to me to decide if I was worthy for the journey. A beautiful moment of surrender followed the tears. I gave God my prejudices against my own gender, my distorted femininity, and surrendered my strength.

That evening, God's voice continued to permeate my heart as He spoke to my brokenness. My perspective had been so far off and it was clear now. I now knew I had been looking at gender issues through a broken lens. The truth was, I was created in the image of God and so were these men and women I was serving alongside. I was humbled before a God who didn't look at our rank, merit and physical prowess as I did. He simply looked for the soul; a soul that would willingly say yes to His vision and calling and step out in faith.

My encounter with God freed me from the bondage of pride and self-condemnation and the burden of years of fruitless striving. It reminded my redeemed heart that my priceless value was found firmly in the hand of my Creator. I knew I had not earned the grace that God poured so endlessly into my life. Could I somehow make myself any more worthy of carrying out the task before me? No. So, I knelt before my God, not as a woman and a soldier, but as a wholly loved child, and spoke the word *yes* – *yes* to my gender, *yes* to my calling and *yes* to my Lord.

In May, I prepared to push out into the unfamiliar waters and move to the east coast, my first permanent relocation since arriving in Washington on a snowy January evening in 2009. It amused me to look back on my first expedition as a newly minted officer, when everything I owned fit in the back of my Jeep and I didn't know how to march and salute at the same time. The military life I was about to start living was mostly a mystery to me and my attitude was anxious and ambitious. I was hungry to learn and equally clueless as to how to do anything, aside from wear my uniform correctly and run a decently fast two-miler. I had big dreams and big fears. Countless, unforeseen trials waited for me and I made A LOT of mistakes.

But each year, each new job and each promotion brought with it grateful retrospection and awareness of growth, like the penciled-in height chart my mom marked on a wall in our childhood home each birthday. I couldn't help but look back on the past four years with a sense of satisfaction of progress and an exhale of relief. Thank God that I've come this far. Now let's move on.

⛰

I spent a greater part of my final Saturday morning in Washington in conversation with my sweet friend, Mary. She is a kindred spirit who always seems to bring out things in the depths of my heart when we talk. At one point she asked me about my impending move, if it would be hard for me to leave. A flood of memories and emotions that were so intertwined with the past four and a half years of my life seemed to pour out of me. But above all, I saw the goodness of God and His hand covering my life.

I began to summarize my experiences, thinking back to when I first came to Washington. Fresh out of college and brand new to life on my own, I was plagued with insecurities and lack of self-confidence. To add to the mix, I was thrown into my first real job in the military, which included leading soldiers into combat just a few short months after arriving. My first tour in Afghanistan was fraught with anxiety from constantly traveling IED-laden roads, burnout from working seven days a week and the palpable darkness from manipulative and distrustful working relationships. I returned home hardened, bitter and deeply confused by the things I had experienced. My faith was floundering. I believed that God had hidden His face from me. Nothing in my life seemed to make sense then, and I thought my apathy towards God and distorted view of grace meant that He could no longer use me.

After six months of stumbling around in the dark and plugging my ears to the whisper of God, I gave up. Sometimes God takes time and teaches us to exercise our faith and patience as He works on us. And sometimes, He just flips on the light switch and dumps His blessings on our surprised souls, like a bucket of cold water over our dusty heads. I cried out to God in an act of surrender. He stepped out of the shadows, where He had been waiting for me to call out His name, and destroyed the demons of inferiority and oppression – a two-year plague. I felt like Paul in the Bible, scales falling from his eyes as he awakened a new man in the presence of the living God. My past fell away and the invincible future lay before me.

Over the next several months the Lord opened doors and windows and kicked down walls to pour out His goodness into my heart. I asked Him for *more* from my life and He gave me more, and then some. Just weeks after I closed out a year of blessing and big dreaming, I departed for my second trip to Afghanistan. I could have never imagined how God would write my story there.

The first five months of my deployment I was betrayed and ostracized, forced into the center of a senseless witch hunt. I had never felt so utterly alone and despised. My heart hurt, and I was tempted, as I so often am, to pull into my shell and isolate myself from the pain, other people and from God. Thankfully next I remembered the words I had written months earlier, when I first arrived in country.

"Last night I was reminded that I am never alone; that God has gone before me and goes with me and behind me to make a way for my life. I am never forsaken and never without purpose."

My feeble faith clung to the promise that God would never let go of me. Then, He completely shifted the second half of the deployment, sending success and innumerable blessings my way. He surrounded me with incredible people who treated me as an equal and let me have a whole lot of fun. This time as I returned home to the U.S., I did so with a soul at rest, knowing God was fighting for me. Since returning home, I felt more whole, calmer and more like myself than ever. The favor of God continued to rest over my head as I walked with Him. I didn't fear the future, because I knew God had rooted me in Himself and continued to walk before me as I moved on to a new phase of life.

When I finished telling Mary what my Lord had done in my time here in Washington, she told me that it was as if *the Lord had given me this season of my life in a package.* The more I thought about it, the more it seemed to be true. I did feel calm and resolved now, with no loose ends or unfinished work. God had brought my heart back into step with His. He'd handed me a beautifully wrapped package I could carry with me as I went forward. Not baggage or a burden, but a *gift,* a visible symbol of restoration and redemption.

I wasn't afraid of moving on, for I knew who went before me and with me and protected me from the past that may try to haunt me. I was highly favored, richly blessed, *never forsaken and never without purpose.*

Chapter 25

The Battlefield

I arrived at Fort Lee, Virginia on June 2, 2013 after a long day of driving straight through from Illinois where I had spent two days catching up with my family and picking up my cat, Finn. I signed into the Army Logistics University, where I would spend the next six months sitting in a classroom learning everything I needed to know about Army logistics. Though I wasn't crazy about the prospect of classroom drudgery, I was looking forward to plenty of free time to run and explore local historic sites. I set up home in a small apartment just outside of the Petersburg National Battlefield, where General Grant and his Union Forces sieged and eventually defeated General Lee's band of Confederates during the Civil War. It was fascinating and sobering to be so close to such a key part of American History and reminded of the country's heartbreaking past.

Virginia welcomed me with a crashing thunderstorm and dripping humidity. After the rain cleared, I laced up my running shoes and found a wooded trail near the battlefield and began a suffocating slog through the midday heat. Looking at my watch, I groaned, seeing my painfully slow pace in large white numbers on my wrist. I willed my body up and down the hilly twists and turns for three miles before calling it quits and returning to the air-conditioned comfort of my apartment, making a mental note to run earlier in the day. I found myself already missing the mild Washington summer.

Classes started days later, and I found myself in a packed auditorium of 150 of my peers, awaiting our initial in-briefing and classroom assignments. None of the faces looked familiar to me, but that didn't matter. I was comfortable being alone and wasn't super eager to make new friends between then and November when we would graduate. After a briefing about expectations the cadre broke the students down into groups of 20. For the first seven weeks, we would be a unit, assigned an instructor for our common core block of classes.

I hated being back in the world of logistics after working with Special Forces in Afghanistan. Many of my CST peers had found their "in" to work in the Special Operations community by transferring to the Civil Affairs branch or getting a coveted job at Fort Bragg after returning home. During deployment I made an attempt to get out of the Army entirely. My service obligation ended in May 2012, so I submitted a packet to my home unit for a release from active duty. I was feeling disillusioned and marginalized and didn't want to be a part of the machine any longer.

The Army felt like a bad boyfriend to me – always promising a new assignment or posting with the opportunity for bigger and better things and always disappointing. I blindly held on to the expectation that it *would* get better, that I would have a great boss who saw me as an asset rather than a reliability because of my gender, or that my talents would finally get put to good use. Army culture wasn't where I fit in, yet I always wanted to feel like I truly belonged. Finally, mid deployment in 2012 I came to the realization that things were probably as good as they were going to get career-wise, so I tried to get out of the Army. But, just days later I received orders sending me to the Combined Logistics Captains Career Course at Fort Lee, and due to a paperwork error, my packet to leave the Army was never signed or approved. I was stuck for at least three more years. Needless to say, I just wanted to get through the logistics course and be on my way. I saw it as an inevitability rather than an opportunity and put forth minimal effort to get by each day.

We started our first full day of class with a six-page quiz to test our baseline knowledge of the Military Decision-Making Process and other Army doctrine. I whizzed through the quiz, barely paying attention to the answers I was circling. That was my style of test taking, and thus far in my life it had served me sufficiently. Afterwards, our instructor collected our tests and handed them out again randomly for peer grading. *Tyler Mathis*, the top of the test read. *Who is that?* I thought to myself, looking around. Whoever this *Tyler Mathis* was, he was smart, missing only three questions in the quiz. I rolled my eyes. *Show off.* Someone handed me back my packet. I had missed more than fifteen answers, which made me feel irritated and slightly embarrassed. I scanned the name tapes in the room for *Mathis* and finally found him to give him back his quiz. *How old is this guy?* I thought as we made eye contact. He looked like he couldn't be more than 18, but was a captain nonetheless. Wordlessly I handed him back his quiz and sat down.

Our instructor, a sexist-against-her-own-gender Army Captain, divided us into tables of six and started up a cheesy icebreaker game. Tyler sat across from me and we casually chatted before realizing we were both from Illinois. He had grown up in Moline, just a couple hours up the road from my hometown and had gone to college in state. I hadn't hardly met anyone in the Army from Illinois, much less anyone who had heard of my small hometown, Mahomet. Over the next few weeks we bonded over our shared home state and our irrational fear of sharks, and he talked incessantly about the Chicago Blackhawks, who were playing in (and eventually won) the Stanley Cup finals that summer.

Just days earlier, a man I had been dating cut off contact with me, saying he didn't feel anything towards me and that he never thought of me as his girlfriend. I had blindly been in a one-way relationship for six months, thinking this upstanding Christian man was the one I was going to marry. I felt broken-hearted and angry at him for leading me on, then foolish for letting my heart run away with me. For several weeks I grieved the loss and took to the battlefield to run my pain into God's hands. Behind the cover of sunglasses I cried, my tears mingling with the salty rivers of sweat dripping down my face. I wrote the words of 1 Peter 1:6 on a notecard and taped it to my mirror as a reminder of God's faithfulness. *So be truly glad. There is wonderful joy ahead, even though you must endure many trials for a little while.* Every mile I ran that summer felt like a battle against despair, and I knew that God would transform my grief into joy. He was trustworthy with my heart, and I clung to His promises.

One day in mid-July, after class I had the opportunity to share some of my photos of Afghanistan with a few of my classmates. I had talked a little about the CST program and deployment and shared some of my experiences at the request of a few of my peers. Our instructor had left for the afternoon, but we had to stay in the classroom until a designated time to avoid rousing the suspicion of other instructors that she left early. With my laptop in view, I clicked through albums of photos from 2012, talking about the VSO mission as I went with my classmate audience. Proudly I showed photos of Lynn and I in the bazaar on patrol, Schester, our beloved working dog and I, shooting an AK-47 against the backdrop of mountains in Paktika, and village kids with henna-tinted hands. Smiling, I remembering the better times after Lynn and I started working together. I skipped over mentioning Haley. The experience was still too painful and I couldn't recount the stories about her without bitterness.

Suddenly and without warning, the room heaved and tilted, spinning violently, and I crumpled to the floor beside my chair. I didn't know which way was up and the spinning wasn't subsiding. My classmates sprung into action, folding a uniform top underneath my head and pointing a fan towards me to cool me off. Someone grabbed an instructor from a nearby classroom and called an ambulance. I covered my eyes with my hands and prayed the vertigo would stop. The inexplicable experience was frightening and I couldn't move, on top of the embarrassment of having an audience of 15 peers watching me in a vulnerable state, whimpering on the floor. Paramedics arrived quickly with a stretcher and took my vitals while I lay on the floor, still unable to move. If I didn't open my eyes or move my head the spinning would mostly subside.

"Do you think maybe you're just anxious?" one of the paramedics asked as he pricks my finger to check my blood sugar. "We see this all the time when people are stressed out." This didn't feel like stress or low blood sugar. I kept trying to explain that I wasn't lightheaded and dizzy. The room was actually spinning, like my inner ear was doing cartwheels. The medics stood me up on my feet to take a second blood pressure reading, and the whirling began again. My knees buckled and the men hoisted me on to the gurney. I closed my eyes as they wheeled me down the long hall to the fourth-floor elevators, past open classroom doors and gawking officers and instructors.

In the emergency room I sat slumped over in a wheelchair for two hours, waiting to be seen by a doctor, totally unable to hold my head upright. The spinning had subsided and was replaced by a funhouse mirror effect. Everything around me was rocking and waving, and my head felt thick and dull. I winced against the bright fluorescent lights. Soon, my instructor burst through the hospital doors looking irritated, no doubt for being busted for leaving the classroom early and having a student have a medical emergency.

"Morris, you pregnant?" she asked in a huff.

"No, I'm not." I answered, irritated.

"You sure?" she pressed, unconvinced. I glared back and didn't answer. Gratefully, a bed opened up in a back room, and a nurse came to wheel me back.

"You want me to stay with you, Morris?" my instructor asked, looking as if she hoped I'd say no. I declined her offer and closed my eyes, wishing she would just leave.

No answers for my vertigo came that evening or in the weeks that followed. Provider after provider and specialist after specialist handed me off to the next person, unable to offer a diagnosis or insight into my now constant vertigo. I missed hours of classroom instruction, unable to hold my head up or stay awake. Every day I was still miserably dizzy, and the medicine the doctors gave me to help with the spinning made me slow and drowsy. The fluorescent classroom lights were nearly unbearable, and when I wasn't in total darkness I had to move around with my hands clamped over my eyes, peeking through my fingers to keep the painful light out. My head and sinuses felt like a balloon was being inflated from the inside of my skull and a dense brain fog made it impossible to think straight. Every time I tried to eat, a wave of nausea would sweep over me mid-bite and I would drop my fork and trudge to the couch to lay down.

Despite my misery, I forced myself to keep running, only taking a few days off here and there if my vertigo became unbearable. Day after day in the soaking summer humidity I put one foot in front of the other, willing my body and brain into submission across the Petersburg battlefield. When the vertigo got bad during a run I would close my eyes for seconds at a time or clamp my hand over my eyes to block out as much sun as possible. My brain felt dangerously overstimulated, like it was going to short circuit at any moment. But as I ran, I continued to hold tightly to God's promise that there were days of great joy ahead, even though they felt so far away in the midst of an unrelenting and mysterious illness.

One afternoon I cried to my mom out of frustration. I felt like I couldn't catch a break, going from deployment to a devastating breakup to major illness.

"Meredith, I just have this feeling that God is really pleased with you," she said over the phone. "I don't know what it is, I just sense He's pleased with you and your heart and how you've trusted Him during this time." I cried harder, feeling like my heart and body were in messy pieces which I was struggling to put together. My hope that God had a plan and purpose for my trials were the only things keeping me anchored in the midst of my struggles.

One particularly rough evening I texted Tyler, who had become my closest friend in our class, and told him I was dizzy and feeling scared. Within seconds he was in his truck driving to my apartment to be with me. That night he sat with me for two hours, talking to distract me while I rested my spinning head against the couch cushions, afraid to move an inch. My Maine Coon cat, Finn, swished his tail around Tyler's ankles and eventually curled up on the couch between us. He would tell me some weeks later that he had been sweating profusely in my overly warm apartment and that he was allergic to cats. I gasped and laughed, appreciating every bit of his willingness to just be with me in my moment of need.

Our friendship grew over the weeks and soon we were spending nearly every day after class together. The very first time we hung out I invited myself over to his apartment watch Shark Week. I didn't have cable, but I knew Tyler did, and a big screen TV to boot. Somehow, I cajoled an invite out of him, and we laughed and screamed over ridiculous shark specials for the evening. He made me tofu tacos for our very first dinner together, and his efforts warmed my heart more than I let on. I was a vegan at the time and Tyler would scour the internet for recipes to cook for dinner. Almost every night he would whip up a meal while I lay on his couch, dizzy and miserable, a blanket over my face to block the light. At least once a week he would drive me 45 minutes to Richmond so I could buy my favorite vegan cupcakes at the Whole Foods there, knowing I struggled with driving more than a few minutes at a time.

Tyler was a steady, reliable friend over our six months stationed together. I felt privileged to get to know a deeper side of him that our classmates never saw. In class, he was a goofy entertainer who loved a good, riling debate. Our instructor had condescendingly nicknamed him Surfer Boy, implying he was an empty-headed partier. With me he was compassionate and sensitive and a gentle caretaker in my sickest moments. Tyler was intelligent and hardworking and would gladly take the credit for getting me through class. We pulled an all-nighter to finish our final project, which included complex logistics planning for a major national military operation. We ate Oreos together on his couch and watched back to back Tarantino movies until the sun came up, grinding out our papers and presentations together. To this day Tyler will claim that I napped all night while he did the legwork for my presentation.

At the end of the course Tyler and I received our assignments – he would go to Fort Bragg, North Carolina after graduation and I would head to the opposite coast, back to my beloved Joint Base Lewis-McChord, Washington. It felt right, going back to Washington, where my journey first began. That place held a deeply special place in my heart and returning felt like coming home. I had lost and found myself and my faith in that beautiful place, the eternally snow-capped Mt. Rainier as silent witness. No matter how far away I went or how long I was gone, the image of it was always in my mind, looming and wild and majestic. Even when everything about home changed, the mountain was steadfast and unaltered.

Chapter 26

Songbird

When I was a newborn baby my Grandma Dolly gave me the name SONGBIRD, as prophetic blessing over my tiny new life. Years later, she wrote me a letter with the story of my nickname, typed neatly on her typewriter.

When Meredith's grandfather retired from the Air Force, and we moved to our farm in Illinois, he made a wren box for me and put it on the fence post right outside my kitchen window.

Every spring a mother wren had her babies there and I loved to watch her going in and out feeding them. Sometimes, she would sit on top of her little house and sing – her tiny throat vibrating with music as she lifted her head to the sky.

One day, I was sitting at my kitchen table with pad and pencil – thinking about writing a poem about our newborn granddaughter, when the little wren flew by my window – and I smiled and said "pretty little songbird."

My poem had a title and "Songbird" became the nickname for our own pretty little Meredith Anne.

For months after I became sick I struggled to find the courage to write. Flutters of ideas and thoughts came and went through my head, but I neglected to transfer them into type. I felt perpetually uninspired and in the dark. My circumstances sapped the life out of me – like the summer humidity did back at Fort Lee. My training runs in the swampy Virginia heat seemed to mock me to my core. It was a full on war between my body and the elements, and I felt myself losing. I saw marginal improvement over the weeks and months and could never seem to find my stride. Running, which used to bring me so much joy, felt like an elusive friend that I could never find no matter how many miles I ran.

Summer's torture came and went, but fall never brought the fresh inspiration or healing I had been seeking. Frustrations with my illness and my training continued to eat at me. Then I was reminded of something beautiful. My Grandma Dolly sent me one of Oswald Chambers' quotes in an email as a little bit of encouragement. It said, Song birds are taught to sing in the dark, and we are put into the shadow of God's hand until we learn to hear Him."

Months later I was listening to NPR during my early morning commute, and the morning segment Bird Note came on. I started paying attention when I heard the host was talking about songbirds. Despite my namesake, I knew relatively little about them. She began talking about the migrations of songbirds. They migrate almost exclusively at night in total darkness, relying on the moon and stars to show them the way. The cover of darkness keeps them safe from predators and helps them communicate better with the rest of their flock. God was truly teaching me to sing His song, even in the darkness.

I finally realized that I had been looking at my circumstances inappropriately. Darkness does not alter truth. What is visible in the light does not change in the shadows. God's promises do not change in times of trial. His love for me and His goodness have no boundaries. They do not grow or lessen depending on my perception of them or my worthiness to receive them. His character remains constant, even in my darkness.

One October day in 2015 I lay in bed, tears soaking my pillow. For the previous three days I had been experiencing the most frightening and prolonged vertigo since my illness began. The emergency room doctor I had seen in the middle of the night pumped me full of Valium and sent me home to sleep and follow up with a neurologist. I was alone and scared and cried wordless prayers to God, begging Him to help me. Suddenly, right in front of me I saw the gentle face of Jesus. Tears were streaming down His face, and He was weeping along with me, sharing in my suffering. He reached out both of His hands, putting them on the sides of my face, and looked me in the eyes, His own filled with tears.

"I know," He said. "I know." God was there, as present and full as anything I could see. Even if healing wasn't on its way right then, I knew without a doubt that God saw my suffering and His heart hurt right along with mine. He showed himself to me in a way I had never seen or experienced before. God loved me deeply and did not watch His child suffer with a callous heart.

Months passed before I had the courage to write again. I battled a numb cloud of depression and vertigo-induced anxiety. Life lost its color and most days found me in bed sleeping for 12-hour stretches, or with my head buried in my hands in front of my computer at work. I wasn't getting any healthier, or any closer to a diagnosis. At first, I stopped asking God for healing and answers and merely prayed for the strength to get by. Then I stopped praying for anything at all, accepting my health condition as a permanent fixture in my life.

In March of 2016, just three months after God spoke to me in my car about seeing the Mountain again, I attended a healing combat veteran's program at Boulder Crest Retreat in Bluemont, Virginia. For the first time in a long time I felt a little flame of hope rekindle in my heart. That week I started writing again, reclaiming my *Songbird* namesake, knowing there was life and healing ahead. This is the poem I wrote.

Little Bird

*Her cold body melds to the ground, the outline of her frozen
wings barely showing through the snow. The trees above,
leafless and quiet, stand like sentinels witnessing her struggle,
then stillness. Her faint heartbeat marches on, heard only by the
rattling wind and the ancient trees.
The earth beneath her senses and stirs, thawing from winter's
long slumber.*

*The little bird remains, aware but unmoving as life breathes,
gently at first, then assuredly.
The sun searches tentatively for her face, filtering through the
newly budded branches.
The little bird feels her heart begin to beat, steady and sure,
moving lifeblood into her wings.
She hears the sun whisper, "little bird, you are meant for the
skies," gently, lovingly.*

193

*As the little bird struggles to open her eyes, her heart flutters at
the sight of the blooming woods.
Far above her head, over the sun-dappled treetops, familiar
calls beckon her upward toward the warm sky. On feeble legs
she tests her stiff wings, cold and rigid from winter's long night.
The little bird fears the unfamiliarity of leaving her cold place
on the ground, but the sun whispers again, "Little bird, you are
meant for the skies."*

*With clenched eyes she flaps her unsure wings and vaults
herself towards the treetops, higher and higher. As she breaks
through the leaves into the blinding sun, the little bird snaps
open her eyes. The familiar calls are all around her now. She
meets the gazes of the other birds, spiraling and diving in the
blue sky. With melodies of a thousand songs in her heart and
golden sun on her wings she flies. As she soars she hears the
sun whisper, "Little bird, you are meant for the skies."*

Epilogue

Tyler and I eloped on September 24, 2014, on Waikiki Beach, Hawaii, just a week before his second deployment to Afghanistan. We spent the next 14 months apart, finally moving in together for the first time in November 2015 when Tyler left the Army after six and a half years of faithful service. Two months after his service ended, the Army began the process to medically retire me for chronic vertigo. After eight and a half years of active duty, I hung up my uniform for good. Together Tyler and I navigated our way into civilian life and put our roots down in Washington, under the watchful eye of the mountain.

As I'm writing this, Tyler is asleep next to me in our bed, our dog PJ curled up between us while a cool summer night breeze drifts in through the open window. I look back on our journey together the past five years and am overwhelmed with gratitude for how far we've come together and God's immense faithfulness. He will tell you that on the first day of class back at Fort Lee, Virginia, he picked me out in a room full of 150 people and knew I'm going to marry that girl. It took me a little while longer to come to the same realization, but I'm so glad I did!

Healing from my illness still hasn't come, but I know that it will. Perhaps for the first time, I feel ready for it. If I hadn't been sick and booted from the Army, this book would never have happened. Without an 18-month stretch of unemployment that followed my discharge, there's no way I would have been quiet enough to hear God's voice when He told me to write. So, in many ways I'm grateful for the struggle and uncertainty, because it only highlights the goodness and perfect timing of a God with higher ways than mine.

I struggled with a few parts of this book, wondering how much I should share of the deeply painful moments of my story. I hadn't openly spoken about my abuse to anyone in my family outside of my husband, and only a few other people knew the dark extent of it.

"I think you need to put it in your book," Tyler told me. "Your story can help other women like you who have been through the same stuff." I was wavering, wondering if I could just write about Capt. Andrews' verbal and emotional abuse and leave out the other gory details. Somehow, shame still had a hold on me. But, I realized that not sharing the extent of my struggle would diminish God's incredible, restorative mercy. Only hours earlier I received word that Capt. Andrews had been arrested and convicted of aggravated rape of a teenage girl a few years prior, earning him a dishonorable discharge from the Army and time in prison. My heart broke, and I wept for her and for my younger self. Shame had kept me in the dark for too long, and it had to go. So, with Tyler's encouragement and support, I wrote it in.

The process of forgiving Capt. Andrews and Haley, the two biggest offenders, has been long and ongoing. It took years for me to finally understand the depth of their hurt and brokenness in their individual lives and begin to let go of their offenses against me. And more than anything, I've had to learn to forgive myself for the past and not let shame overshadow God's restorative grace. There are days when regrets about the past and vindictive bitterness rear their ugly heads in my heart, which my sister Lydia aptly calls shame attacks. I have to continually accept the healing mercy of a God who deeply cares for my heart and thank Him for what He's done for me. On the days when I especially feel ensnared by anger, I pray for Capt. Andrews and Haley. It's gut-wrenchingly hard to do, because I'd rather justify my anger than surrender it. But, His love is big enough to redeem their stories, too. My hope as this book goes out into the big world is that my vulnerability in sharing my story will give others the freedom to do the same and to know they are not alone. Shame loses its power in the light of truth and authenticity. And I hope that people will more clearly see the face of God in their struggles and know they are never forsaken and never without purpose – God does not abandon His children! If there's one thing I know about God, it's that He is a God of restoration, taking the most broken pieces of our lives and redeeming them for good. He is always faithful to us.

The Mountain Still Stands

Let the fog lift, let the clouds fade into the sky.
The Mountain still stands, looming and sure.
Through the night and the storm.
Morning breaks through the dark, warming the cold.
Black skies turn blue, then pink, singing morning's song.
The world wakes and warms in the clear day.
The Mountain is there, as it always has been.

ACKNOWLEDGEMENTS

So many people deserve heartfelt thanks for making this book possible. First and foremost, thank you to Deborah McLain and Creative Force Press for your immense support, prayers and encouragement throughout this process, and helping make my vision a reality. When we met eight years ago at worship team practice, I never expected we'd be where we are now! Thank you to my husband Tyler for your endless support and for taking care of our little family during my time of productive and not so productive unemployment. I'm so grateful for your passionate insights and the way you refuse to let shame and insecurity find a place in my life. I love you more than I could adequately express. You're truly my greatest gift.

Thank you to my wonderful family, mom and dad, Lydia, Laura, Madeline, Aunt Jan, Uncle Rex, Uncle Kevin, Aunt Jill, Grandma, Grammy, and mom and dad Mathis for your love, your excitement, for reading and sharing my writings over the years, and for believing that my story was important and worth telling.

Thank you to my friends who have spoken truth and courage into my heart over the years, playing bigger roles in this story than you could ever imagine: Mary McEvoy, Ashley Ramirez, Lynn Powers, Camille Effler, Alex Horton, Keesha Dentino, Samantha Moeller, Mussarat Assam, Fareeha Ali, Lori Kuyt, Katie and Tyler Minton, Crystal Wade, Wendy DiVico, Katie and Aaron Payne, Trisha Ferguson, Krista Dunk, Stephanie Parisi, Krista Tilford, Steve McLain, Daniel and Treasa Sabo, and the wonderful humans at Boulder Crest Retreat, Capital Christian Center, and Woodland Church.

And to many who prayed endlessly for me and my soldiers through two combat deployments, sending notes of encouragement and life-giving packages, I'm indebted to your kindness and wish I could personally thank each and every one of you. Finally, thank you to the men and women in the arena who fight the good fight: soldiers and leaders of 5/2 Stryker Brigade Combat Team who endured hell during OEF 09-11, the brave women of CST 3, Special Squad of Paktika Province, and my brothers of ODA 1112 and ODA 1416. You are all truly heroes. Thank you for your service.

ABOUT THE AUTHOR

Meredith Mathis is a combat veteran who served in the U.S. Army as an officer for eight and a half years before medically retiring in 2016. In 2018, she published her first book through Creative Force Press, *The Mountain Still Stands: A Young Soldier's Battle for Peace in a Time of War.*

Meredith lives in Lacey, Washington with her husband, Tyler, and their two dogs, Ruby and PJ. She is the owner of Songbird Studio, which specializes in photo restoration and digital archiving.

The Mountain Still Stands is proudly published by:

Creative Force Press

www.CreativeForcePress.com

Do You Have a Book in You?

24003494R00111

Made in the USA
Columbia, SC
19 August 2018